Access for All

K. H. SCHAEFFER
AND ELLIOTT SCLAR

Access for All

Transportation and
Urban Growth

New York   Columbia University Press

Library of Congress Cataloging in Publication Data

Schaeffer, K H
    Access for all.

    Includes bibliographical references and index.
    1. Urban transportation. 2. Urbanization. 3. So-
ciology, Urban. I. Sclar, Elliott, joint author.
II. Title.
HE305.S3 1980   388.4   80-21520
ISBN 0-231-05164-6
ISBN 0-231-05165-4 (pbk.)

Columbia University Press
New York   Guildford, Surrey

Columbia University Press Morningside Edition 1980

This edition reprinted by arrangement with Penguin-Viking

Printed in the United States of America

CONTENTS

LIST OF FIGURES

LIST OF MAPS

LIST OF TABLES

The point we make in *Access for All* is a simple one. The quality of human life depends on the amount of access we have to one another. We must have contact to exchange goods and services as well as joys and sorrows. People need to be brought together to take advantage of the economies of scale in industry. Cities exist as a spatial solution to the problem of improving contact or access among people. By colocating activities of work and community living it is possible to increase access. While increased mobility can, under certain conditions, lead to increased access, mobility and access are not the same. It is this concept which has been overlooked at severe costs to our metropolitan areas. This is the message of *Access for All*.

In our drive to escape the overcrowded, dirt and noise polluted cities of the nineteenth century, we have substituted mobility for colocation. The result is that by the 1970s we achieved the most mobility of any people ever to inhabit this planet, but our access to one another showed signs of deterioration. The quality of life started to unravel at the seams. Our argument was then, when we wrote the book, and is today that more mobility will not solve the problem, but only make it worse. The automobile has reached the limit in its ability to enhance access. What is needed is the development of balanced metropolitan land use patterns which foster access without excess mobility or excess crowding.

When we drafted this book the first energy crisis was still in the future. Our ideas were out of step with the conventional wisdom among "transportation experts." The judgment prevailed that the good life meant ever more thinly populated metropolitan areas with increased mobility through high-speed automobile travel over ever longer distances.

By the time we reviewed the copyedited version of the first edition the energy crisis of 1973–74 had passed. As we suggested

(p. 176), its impacts were significant but minimal. More people were seeing a new wisdom in clustered housing, condominiums, inner-city living, mass transit, and auto-free zones.

As the rerelease of this book proceeds we have had another gasoline shortage and continuing increases in petroleum prices far above general inflationary pressures. For economic reasons much of what we advocate has become common wisdom, though many continue to believe that the preferred societal solution remains the one-family home on large plots of land connected by uncrowded freeways on which cars can travel at high speeds.

We therefore find it imperative to point out that, regardless of whether society can economically afford a more dispersed life style, the current trends toward colocation and greater reliance on mass transit are necessary, if the desired end is an enhanced life style which balances the individual's desires for privacy with those for community. Simply stated, more access and less mobility ought to be viewed not as depressing our standard of living, but rather enhancing it.

K. H. Schaeffer
Elliott Sclar
April 1980

PREFACE

Books with multiple authors inevitably raise the questions: Who contributed what? Whose ideas are these? Many of our ideas began to develop when Schaeffer became involved with transportation planning studies which proposed new facilities but dodged the questions of need and impact and when Sclar wrote his doctoral dissertation on the public financing of transportation in the Boston area. In preparation of the manuscript, Schaeffer wrote the first draft of Chapters 1, 2, 3, 4, 9 and 10, and Sclar of Chapters 5 and 6. Chapter 7, 'The Social Crisis', was written by Schaeffer and Chapter 8, 'The Economic Crisis', by Sclar.

In writing the manuscript we received suggestions, encouragement and assistance from many people, amongst them Matthew Edel, Norman Faramelli, Donald MacDonald and Clyde Rogers. Though we borrowed their ideas freely, naturally we are solely responsible for any errors or misconceptions the book contains. We also want to thank Nancy Lyons, who read the entire manuscript and whose extremely cogent comments helped to untangle confused thoughts and sentences. We greatly appreciate the care with which Lou Robinson drew the maps and figures for the book and with which Gayle Bowden and Elaine Gordon typed the many drafts. Last, but not least, we want to acknowledge the steady support of our wives, especially when the going got rough and nothing worked right.

ACKNOWLEDGEMENTS

The authors and publishers wish to thank the following for kind permission to reproduce in this volume from the works cited:

Harvard University Press for the map of 'Boston, Cambridge and Their Environs in the 17th Century' drawn by Erwin Raisz for Samuel Eliot Morison, *Harvard College in the 17th Century* (Copyright © 1936 by the President and Fellows of Harvard College, 1964 by Samuel Eliot Morison); for a quotation from Carl Seaburg and Stanley Paterson, *Merchant Prince of Boston: Colonel T. H. Perkins, 1764–1854* (Copyright © 1971 by the President and Fellows of Harvard College); and for a quotation from Sam B. Warner, Jr, *Street Car Suburbs, The Process of Growth in Boston, 1870–1900* (Copyright © 1962 by the President and Fellows of Harvard College).

Harper & Row, Publishers, Inc., for a quotation from Arnold Gesell and Frances L. Ilg, *The Child from Five to Ten*, Harper & Row, N.Y., 1946, page 443; and for a quotation from Arnold Gesell, Frances L. Ilg, Louise Bates Ames, *Youth: The Years from Ten to Sixteen*, Harper & Row, N.Y., 1956, pages 496–7.

William Morris Agency for a quotation from Fred Allen, *Much Ado About Me*, Little, Brown & Company, 1956.

The City of Edmonton, City Planning Department, for use of planning and transit system maps from the General Plan, Office Consolidation, 1972

Access for All

CHAPTER 1

Introduction

That there is something severely amiss with transportation in our cities and metropolitan areas is one of the most widely recognized problems of the man-made environment. In one form or another, everyone has experienced the transportation 'problem' and in one form or another most have a favorite 'solution' for it. Some advocate more highways, others more public transportation. Some want to ban cars, others drinking and accident-prone drivers. Some blame the over-sized trucks, others the taxis and buses. Some want public transportation to be free, others insist that it is self-supporting. Some hope for electric cars, others for 'personal rapid transit' and 'dial-a-ride'. Some advocate special roads for buses, others more expressways restricted to private cars. With as visible a problem as traffic jams, accidents, unreliable public transportation and spiraling costs, as well as air and noise pollution and such a wide spectrum of solutions, literally hundreds of books have been devoted to all aspects of the urban transportation problem. With this wide selection to choose from, why, the weary reader might ask, do we need another book? What do you, Schaeffer and Sclar, have to say that has not been said before?

In our concerns for the subject, and in our reading of the literature, we have found many more 'solutions' than analyses of how the transportation problem arose in the first place. Such pat answers as 'too much congestion', 'too many cars', 'too many people', 'too much wealth', certainly do not lead to solutions for the problem. Unless we understand how we got into the urban transportation débâcle, we will never be able to formulate effective solutions to lead us out of the present morass. It is to this proposition that this book is dedicated.

Urban life is bound up with and predicated on transportation. Cities and metropolitan areas cannot exist without transportation, for its citizens produce neither the food they eat nor the raw materials they consume. With the automobile, transportation, which once was a scarce commodity, has been transformed into one that exists in abundance, and this new-found wealth has affected the entire gamut of life. Regardless of how people turn and twist, nearly every aspect of their lives has undergone changes directly traceable to the existence of the automobile and its big brother the truck. Most of these changes have alleviated past problems, but they have also caused new ones. Life today, from the mother's rush to the hospital to the final trip in the hearse, is touched by transportation, and this usually means the auto, the bus or the truck. Before children are old enough to toddle, they are experienced travelers; there is the trip home from the hospital, to the doctor and to grandma's house, and to parties their parents attend while they sleep soundly or cry lustily in their carrying baskets. Then come the shopping trips with mother and the great 'events', the outings to the zoo, to a picnic and to the swimming pool. By the time children have reached school age, they are daily commuters, some on foot with special guards to keep the cars at bay, but ever more likely by bus. The one- and two-room school houses have disappeared. Schools, even at the elementary level, have become so large that they serve areas – at least in the suburbs – which are too extensive for all children to be expected to walk to school. School administrators and educators feel that these larger schools can offer the student more economically and efficiently the education their interests and talents demand than was possible in the one- and two-room school houses of yesteryear. Educators are not the only ones who have found in the automobile a means to give better or more economical service. For all practical purposes, the physician's housecall has disappeared. Travel for the sick by private car, taxi or ambulance represents a minimal hazard compared to more competent diagnosis and treatment doctors can offer with the tools available at their offices or in a hospital. With the housecall went the peddler, the milkman and the other regularly scheduled door-to-door delivery services. People do not care to select their goods from the limited wares these merchants have to offer if they can more easily and at lower cost select their purchases from the wide displays at a supermarket or department store, and tote them home by automobile.

The automobile has not just changed the manner in which home environment is structured, it has also had major impacts on the home-work relationships. Once people lived in the cities or towns where they also worked. Then, under the influence of the commuter train and the streetcar, some moved to the suburbs and commuted to the city. When the car became common, this trickle became a rush. More and more people moved to the suburbs and increasingly more commercial and industrial businesses followed suit. Today, at least in the United States, more people live in the suburbs than the central cities, and the vast majority of all workers no longer reside in the city or town in which they work. By now, the flight to suburbia has passed its peak, and one would expect that with this passing a balance in transportation has been achieved. But this is not the case. It is true that in recent years travel in and out of the central cities of the United States has been relatively stable both by private car and public transportation, but in the suburbs automobile travel and ownership has increased at a far faster rate than growth in population or income would suggest. This trend is independent of the economic growth cycle, for in periods of unemployment and recession the traffic counts climb as rapidly as during good times. People in search of employment are straying ever further from their residences. When families first move to suburbia from the central city or from other parts of the country, they select a suburb that is within easy reach of their employment. They buy a home and settle down, make friends with their neighbors, and become used to the local schools and stores. When a job change becomes necessary – particularly because of a lay-off – there is every tendency not to move, but to find a job somewhere in the metropolitan area even if it means a longer and less convenient commute. With homes full of labor-saving devices, more and more wives are seeking employment. These working couples are particularly likely to own two cars and to avoid a move should one become unemployed.

Where the metropolitan area is crisscrossed by limited-access super-highways, commutes of fifty miles hardly raise an eyebrow. The Los Angeles area is full of people who live in the San Fernando Valley and work in the electronic and aircraft plants of Orange County, and people who live in identical houses and subdivisions in Orange County who commute through the entire smog-covered Los Angeles basin to identical jobs in the electronic and aircraft plants of the San Fernando Valley. And this is true not just of Angelinos. The residents of the other metropolitan areas behave no differently. There are literally hundreds of thousands of workers all over the United States who commute from one sprawling end of their metropolitan area to the other, and the number of these workers is steadily and inexhaustibly on the increase.

The automobile has given marvelous mobility to those who can own and drive a car. These people can drive past neighborhoods by the dozen which are just like their own, and scores of plants and offices which have jobs just like their own, until, after forty-five to ninety minutes of producing and breathing pollution, they reach their work benches and desks. Since the automobile has freed them from any fixed home–work location over an area of several thousand square miles, hardly any two of them can share their trip to work. Not only do ever more workers commute by car, but most do it as auto drivers. By 1970, in Los Angeles County, 77 per cent of all workers commuted as auto drivers, and of the over half a million workers who live in Orange County, just to the east of Los Angeles, 85 per cent or seventeen in twenty commuted as auto drivers. About half of the remainder were auto passengers, while the rest used public transportation, walked to work or worked at home.

Some of the prices that must be paid for this new-found mobility are well known. There is, first of all, the much discussed and roundly cursed congestion on our highways and byways. Still, this price is more apparent than real. In spite of the frustration of drivers who seek the open road but find only slowly rolling 'parking lots', the automobile even at its worst provides auto drivers today far greater mobility than their forefathers could imagine. Then, there is the price of air pollution, but here again the price is exaggerated. Though there is no doubt that pollution created by the automobile can shorten the lives of those with respiratory ailments, the densely crowded cities of yesteryear with their horse manure and the accompanying insects were not a particularly healthy environment either. There is also the very real price in traffic crashes and killings. While on a per mile basis the auto may be safer than the dray or carriage pulled by temperamental horses, people travel so much more today than then that traffic injuries and deaths have become an ever-present tragedy. Finally, there are the gaping holes the automobile-associated bills create in the family's pocketbook. Automobiles may be fun but they are certainly expensive to buy, to own, to operate and to maintain.

Still, all these prices pale into insignificance by comparison with the social and economic costs society incurred through the loss of access which excessive reliance on the automobile has generated, even though people buy cars to gain access.

Access is what cities are all about. Man invented cities as an economic and social tool to create easy accessibility through collocation. Economically, many need access to one another to produce and distribute goods efficiently. Socially, people need access between the generations, life styles and economic strata. If there are physical barriers between these groups which prevent incidental and unplanned confrontations, alienation is bound to result. Only through simple, informal access to one another can people alleviate misunderstandings and misconceptions between the generations and social groups of society.

It is our contention that the excessive reliance on the automobile is a major factor in the economic and social problems that confront the post-industrial society. While the auto owner-drivers have great physical mobility, the rest of the population has not. Even in the United States only slightly more than half the people have driver licenses, and these include many who are at an age when the reflexes slow down, that is, people who do not dare to drive on the superhighways or in heavy traffic.

The automobile has given improved mobility primarily to the middle class, middle aged. But these owner-drivers have not merely gained new mobility through the car; they have also rearranged the physical location patterns of society to suit their own private needs, and unwittingly in the process destroyed and severely limited the mobility and access of all others. When walking was the prime mode of urban transportation, there was little difference in the mobility of the young, the middle aged and the elderly, and none between the well-to-do and the poor. Because transportation was equally difficult for all, people avoided it, crowded together, and in the process were forced to rub shoulders with one another. Certainly, it was irritating, but at least each was aware of the other's existence. Only very, very few could isolate themselves to such an extent as to utter about the breadless: 'Let them eat cake.'

With the ease of automobile transportation, many have managed in the post-industrial society to isolate themselves in neighborhoods well stratified by family income, age and life style. Here they have no need to rub shoulders with anyone who is not precisely like themselves, and when they leave these havens they do so preferably in hermetically sealed air-conditioned cars which assure that their privacy will not be invaded even while they travel in the crowd.

For the owner-driver the well-stratified neighborhood may appear as an unmitigated haven, for it assures his privacy, and when he chooses to leave it there is always the car, which permits him to be carried from one haven to the next. For all others, these havens are more like ghettos into which they are shunted without a chance to get out. There are the shut-in housewives of the one-car family crawling the walls waiting for their husbands to come home so they can go out. There are the oldsters on small pensions who must beg, sit and wait for a kind neighbor to take them to the supermarket and help them with the grocery bags, for they cannot afford the higher-priced grocery which will deliver, if there is still such a store in town. Finally, there are the young, who grow up without casually encountering any adults who are younger or older than their parents, who have not the least concept of how their parents earn their living in places they have never seen, except on television; and who are utterly bored in their neighborhoods where there is nothing to do; who must beg their parents to chauffeur them everywhere and who are afraid of the unknown world beyond their neighborhoods. Does anyone wonder that the more insulated a neighborhood is, the more likely its youngsters are to turn to drugs from the sheer fright of living?

That the modern man-made environment has produced people as alienated as the forest-dwelling hermit of ages past is hardly surprising. More surprising are the relatively few 'Let them eat cake' pronouncements. But then, the highly age-and-income stratified society, even in the United States, is barely a generation old and it took centuries before absolute monarchy produced a Marie Antoinette.

Transportation problems are certainly not the only cause for the social ills of today's society; but the excessive reliance on private transportation and the physical location patterns, which can only be supported by private transportation, are necessary – though not sufficient – conditions to produce the alienation and economic ailments of the post-industrial society. Transportation is like the blood stream in the human body. Just as an improperly functioning blood-circulation system affects sooner or later the health of every part of the body, so an improperly functioning transportation system over time affects all aspects of society. A healthy body needs a healthy circulation system, and a healthy society requires a healthy transportation system, that is a transportation system which provides access to all.

This is our thesis. In the remainder of the book we hope to convince our readers of its validity. We show how, prior to mechanized transportation, transportation was so scarce that man was forced into patterns of collocation which on one hand gave the individual no real privacy and on the other hand prevented man from taking full advantage of the economies of scale. With mechanized transportation, society gained all the advantages of privacy and economies of scale it could desire. However, the forces that created this balance were so powerful that they continued the growth and the dispersion of cities until people in their search for privacy are losing the concept of community and the urban environment is becoming uneconomical.

Finally, in the book's last two chapters we venture forth with some transportation and land-use concepts which we feel could lead towards a better balance between privacy and community and may point to an economically more efficient urban environment.

CHAPTER 2

The Walking City

To avoid transportation, some five to ten thousand years ago mankind invented the city. Nobody put it quite that way, but the evidence is overwhelming. They rather said, 'Go to, let us build a city and a tower . . . let us make us a name, lest we be scattered abroad upon the face of the whole earth' (Genesis 11 : 4). Why did people have to collocate on small plots of land, when land was so richly available ? Why did they have to band together into permanent cramped quarters where sanitation was always a problem, unless it was too difficult, too cumbersome to come together suddenly and frequently from scattered dwellings ?

Until the advent of machine-powered transportation, land transportation was a scarce 'commodity', something neither sought nor readily substituted for other solutions. With sturdy legs as the only motive power, people walked and toted their goods, or used animals to do the toting for them. Neither method was efficient. Man can't carry much, and pack animals have other ideas. Reportedly, there exists a bas-relief on one of the earliest Egyptian tombs which depicts three exasperated men trying their best to get a heavy laden ass to move. In the intervening five thousand years, neither the ass nor any other animal has changed its basic attitude towards man's bidding. Up to a point the ass and other animals will cooperate, but when driven too far or too fast, or loaded too heavy, cooperation ceases. Transportation that relies on the muscle power of man or beast is cumbersome, awkward, inefficient and full of vagaries. If at all possible, such transportation is something to be avoided. All the inventions of sleds, axles, suspensions and tracks do not change this basic fact.

The walking city was mankind's answer to these transport problems. People collocated to be together for activities they considered important and for which transportation was too slow and too cumbersome. In turn, they planned and arranged their cities around the general principle of avoiding cumbersome internal transportation, both in terms of the necessary number of trips and the length of these trips. Such marks of the modern city as one-way streets, limited-access roads, or land-consuming road interchanges would have been an anathema to the city planners of the pre-motorized era. Consciously or unconsciously, the planners and builders of the walking cities searched for circulation patterns that assured access for the most essential functions by traveling the least distance. At first glance, a medieval town with its crooked streets may seem an inefficient design. However, if we look more carefully, the crooked street patterns suggest a circle with radial spokes and circumferential routes. Where the town is on or against a hill, the crookedness may result from squeezing as many dwellings into the hillside as possible with the least cutting and filling. To cut and fill, the joy of modern architects and contractors, requires extensive transportation. The earth must be moved hither and yon. This is a backbreaking task if the tools are limited to pick, shovel, wheelbarrow and animal-drawn carts.

Since the need to avoid internal transportation dominates the design of walking cities, differences in layouts arose from differences in topography and the priority the community assigned to various activities, rather than from a people's general cultural environment. For example, the New England village patterns of the seventeenth century were quite different from those of the eighteenth, even though there were few basic social, economic and cultural differences between these communities. What was different was the threat from Indian attack. In the seventeenth century, this was a very real hazard. The villages, like Massachusetts' 'Plimouth Plantation', were compact sets of houses surrounded by a stockade. The fields were outside the fenced area. In the eighteenth-century villages, like Litchfield, Connecticut, or Greenfield, Massachusetts, the houses were spread out along a road or two and each house was surrounded by its own farmland. In Plimouth, being able to assemble the citizens quickly was given priority over providing easy access to work. In Litchfield and Greenfield, the opposite was true. The basic principle underlying the communal design was the same, only the priorities had been altered.

Conversely, cities that differ culturally but have similar transport priorities will create basic city layouts that are remarkably alike. Major trading centers require ready access to intercity transportation and ample warehouse space. Warehouses are most efficiently located near the loading and unloading platforms for intercity shipments. An efficient transport pattern in a walking city also requires housing for the rich merchants and their workers near the market and shipment center. With these general specifications, the Dutch and Japanese arrived at remarkably similar solutions in the layout of their major trading centers, Amsterdam and Osaka. Both cities are on rivers that empty into the ocean. There are canals to increase the waterfrontage. Along the canals and river banks are the warehouses, and beyond them are simple square and rectangular blocks with no special 'status' districts.

Cities need quite different layouts when they are seats of religious or secular power. Here the trade routes are less important than the ability to draw crowds into the city to exemplify the power structure through a show of force and pageantry. Thus, temple and capital cities tended toward radial patterns, with an open public space at the center, where masses of people could assemble and the religious or political rituals could be enacted. While these squares were often used also as market places, especially in the smaller cities, this was hardly their *raison d'être* but an efficient secondary use of an existing facility. Abutting the square was the seat of power, the castle or the temple. To gather the faithful from the surrounding countryside, broad avenues stretched out from the square in all directions. Different social castes and groups that lived in the city were assigned to definite quarters, usually sectors between the avenues. These cities were highly class-conscious and the lesser lords and temples often demanded their own squares and spokes. As a result, there was not only an overall radial pattern, but within this grand pattern there were often larger and smaller radial patterns, each centered on some seat of power. Finally, since dense cities, with questionable sanitation and open peat and wood fires for cooking and heating, had a lot of pollution, the lords located toward the windward, while those who served and supplied them resided toward the lee. In all this the basic cultural foundation was secondary, and urban places as culturally different as classical and renaissance Rome, seventeenth-century Paris, Vienna and Edo (Tokyo) developed layouts that look remarkably alike.

In the walking city space was at a premium, for wasted space meant extra transportation. The streets were uniformly narrow, and the larger the city the more houses crowded the streets. Overhanging upper stories, which effectively shielded the streets from sunlight, abounded everywhere. In cities like Paris and London, houses were even on the major bridges. Within the city, wide streets and parks were unknown until the nineteenth century. Then the railroads and the beginnings of urban transit lowered the value of urban space enough to permit the building of the broad tree-lined boulevards typical of so many major capitals from Paris to Rome, Vienna, Berlin and Buenos Aires. Most city parks also date from this period, except those few which had their beginning as royal hunting preserves well beyond the built-up urban area. Haussmann's well-known and much-copied transformation of Paris under Napoleon III (1852–70) with arterial streets and parks presupposes sufficient transportation to permit the relegation of nearly the entire city center to public and institutional use. Without such transportation, however, any plan for an institutional center surrounded by broad avenues must fail. This can be seen from the strange history of the capital city of the United States, Washington, D.C.

Washington had its beginning in 1790, when the First United States Congress authorized the President to select a location no more than ten miles square on the lower Potomac River as the site for the National Capitol and to formulate plans to 'provide suitable buildings for the accommodation of Congress and the President and for the public offices of the Government of the United States'.[1] Writing in the 1960s, John Reps calls the planning of Washington 'at once an act of faith, a political maneuver, a symbolic gesture, and a remarkable achievement in city planning', and notes that the 'original plan, ably reinforced and slightly modified a century after its establishment, has served well for nearly two hundred years'.

From Reps' perspective there can be little doubt about this. The plan which Charles L'Enfant formulated in 1791 was truly an act of faith and served Washington well in its *second* century. But in its *first* century the city nearly died on it. The distances were just too great to provide convenient access as long as walking was the only means of local transportation.

1. An Act of Establishing the Temporary and Permanent Seat of the Government of the United States, 16 July 1790, 1 Stats 130, as quoted in John W. Reps, *Monumental Washington*, The Planning and Development of the Capitol Center, Princeton University Press, Princeton, N.J., 1967.

L'Enfant's plan separated the President's house and the Capitol by one and a half miles and proposed an open view from one to the other along a 160-foot-wide avenue, a width equal to thirteen freeway lanes. The avenues and streets that led to public buildings were 130 feet wide, and even the narrowest residential street measured 90 feet across. Finally, there was an open mall running from both the President's house and the Capitol to the Potomac River.

The streets could be easily staked out as mud paths, but to build buildings and roads required time and money. Both were in short supply, and for years Washington was little more than a house here, a building there, with muddy roads all over the place. No one needed to be astonished that scorn was heaped upon the 'city' from all sides. Foreign diplomats referred to it as the 'City of Magnificent Distances' and as 'a city of streets without houses'. Charles Dickens, after visiting Washington in 1842 when the city had been the nation's capital for over forty years, noted that buildings were erected 'anywhere, but the more entirely out of everyone's way the better'.

Popularly, one may think of administrators and politicians as paper-shuffling bureaucrats, while in reality they are more likely paper writers and annotators. These two activities require a lot of meetings, coordination and communications. Easy access is the alpha and omega of effective government, and L'Enfant's plan did not provide this access. The plan not only separated Congress from the Executive, it also locked up the President in a mansion – the White House – surrounded by parkland. A practical compromise between L'Enfant's dream and daily government operations was made by building government offices in the President's parkland. By 1821, the Departments of State, Treasury, War and Navy had buildings on the White House grounds. The original buildings have disappeared by now, but today's Treasury Building is still on the White House grounds and still obstructs the open view between Congress and the President, definitely physically but maybe symbolically as well. Though the other departments have left the grounds, today the area includes the executive office building (the 'old State Department' building, but not the 1820 version) and the ever-expanding White House building itself. Similarly, buildings were erected along the mall in front of the Capitol. Whenever the government needed readily accessible office space, construction on the mall occurred.

Until 1900, every few decades successive commissions reaffirmed the old plan and produced the necessary pressures to clean up the clutter. Washington has passed through this cycle roughly three times. We wonder if any of these commissions would have succeeded if in each case improved transportation had not permitted a more expansive capital city.

Yesterday's walking cities were not only more crowded than their modern counterparts, they had also a basically different spatial and social arrangement. The urban population of European cities prior to the industrial revolution was not organized around family units, but rather around household units. These were primarily economic production and consumption units, rather than biological reproduction and nurturing units. The household was a business: a smithery, a bakery, a countinghouse. Naturally, someone owned this business, and he lived there with his wife, small children and all the relatives, apprentices, skilled journeymen, servants and retainers that were needed to make the household enterprise a vital undertaking.

This urban environment of collective life carried along in a single stream all ages and classes, leaving no one time or space for solitude and privacy. At the same time the environment eliminated the need for most of the travel that crowds, today, the urban streets and highways. There were no trips between home and work, and the need for shopping, personal business and business-connected trips were sharply reduced. We have no detailed data on precisely how large these households were, but certainly they were much larger than the modern 'residential unit' with its average of three to four souls. Much of the personal and household business that today requires trip-making was then carried on within the household.

While household arrangements may have seemed 'ideal' in their transport requirements, the setup had severe economic and social deficiencies. The household as a production unit had little capability to adjust its labor force to the shifting workload requirements. At times everyone was probably extremely busy, at others there wasn't much to be done. The household maximum size was also severely limited. There are limits to how many people can work and live under one roof. With the slow but steady technological improvements from about A.D. 1100 on, the economies of scale irrevocably favored increasingly larger business and production units. Another drawback to this household arrangement was the utter lack of privacy. The same people were cramped into the same physical space, day and night. How they must have gotten on each other's nerves!

Many walking cities were surrounded by walls. Originally these walls were erected for defense against marauding bands, neighboring principalities and other real and fancied enemies. Since the city fathers of yesteryear were just as optimistic about growth as any proper Chamber of Commerce, the walls at the time of their building usually encompassed some open space. These actions were justified by noting the cost of moving the walls at a later date and the need for extensive gardening plots to support the city in times of siege. But no matter how far out the walls were built, the actual built-up area consisted of large, abutting or closely spaced houses. Here no space was ever wasted, for to cram everything into the smallest possible space was the natural style of the walking city.

While defense may have been the immediate reason for building the walls, in the long run they took on a different importance. Since the walled city could be entered only at the gates, the gates became convenient devices to control the movements in and out of the city and to exact tolls and taxes. For many cities these revenues were the major source of their income.

Most gates were closed most of the time. A major concern of any urbanite who ventured into the countryside was the fear that he would not get back to the city before the gates were closed, and thus would have to spend the night outside the city. This happened often enough, so that the area in front of the gates became the natural locale for inns, and over time for traders who wanted to avoid the towns' excise taxes. As the need for town walls as protection diminished, the areas before the gates emerged as distinct new urban settlements. This happened even when there was still space to expand inside the walled city. As with most things, these new urban settlements needed a name. The French called them *le faubourg*, the Germans *die Vorstadt*. The English had no special term for them, though Southwark across the Thames from the city of London was a faubourg in all but name.

The generally restrictive city policies were the prime impetus for the development of the faubourgs; thus it is only natural that these communities were mostly settled by those who did not fit into the city's stern patterns. First, there were the innkeepers who wanted to serve the weary travelers that awaited the opening of the gates. Then there were the houses of the small artisans and merchants who could not afford a city household and who mainly served the rural population. Finally, with ever larger city household enterprises, the faubourg became the residence of the workers who could no longer be housed on the proprietor's premises. These were usually the older journeymen who found in the faubourg the space and privacy to establish their own residential households. The city's householders considered the householders of the faubourg to be a much lower class, and this concept invaded the language. The French adjective 'faubourien' and German 'vorstädtisch' connote a working- or lower-middle-class environment.

Walking cities without walls often grew to the extent that not every location within them was readily accessible. Some places were a 'considerable' walk from others, and the city's locational patterns became slightly stratified. The well-to-do householders were apt to occupy the central part of the town, and were in easy walking distance of all activity centers. The lower classes who owned their residences gravitated toward the outskirts, substituting lower ground rents for greater access convenience. This is, however, the sum and substance of the stratification that was determined by transportation. The masses who rented their quarters, whether they were poor or not, could be found anywhere within the city. While some inner-city streets might house mainly the poor, and others the more substantial, which were which was not a function of access.

Walking cities never grew to very large sizes. A concentrated walking city radiating outward from a central focus becomes unmanageable with a population of as few as 30,000 to 50,000. When urban development dictated the massing of more people, the walking city coalesced around several focal points. The faubourg was one approach for creating new focal points, and this was the pattern of Paris and Vienna. Another approach was scattered towns, and this is how London developed. Here several towns each with its own focal point coalesced over time into one urban area. The city of London was the trading center of the area, but not the seat of government. That was Westminster. While they were still walking cities, the two communities merged into one urban area. The London example may be extreme but the joining of Berlin and

Neukölln, or Boston and Roxbury, is not essentially different. Today, under the influence of modern transportation, this form of enlarging urban areas is becoming the most common pattern. Cities melt into each other, and only the sign along the road tells where one ends and the next begins.

The walking city, in all its varied forms, was designed to minimize the requirement for transportation through collocation. At least as long as small household-sized workshops could manufacture as cheaply as large plants, these designs were a success as far as work trips and goods movements were concerned. With the beginning of the industrial revolution, however, the walking city's collocation concept collapsed. Now ever larger factories were required to exploit fully the capital investment tied up in engines and machines. People could not live where they worked. Also the ever-increasing division of labor required that plants specialize in their products, collect their raw materials from an increasing number of sources, and ship their products to ever wider markets. All these activities required transportation, and transportation that was more efficient than a pair of sturdy legs or a team of horses in front of a cart. Until such improved transportation was created, the industrial walking city choked on overcrowded living and work space if not the traffic in the streets.

Socially, the record of the walking city was always mixed. In a spatial sense, it was a great equalizer. Here people from all walks of life had to come into daily face-to-face contact with one another. There was always someone who was either one's elder or one's junior, who had more or less status than oneself. Poverty and wealth, age and youth, were issues to be dealt with daily and directly rather than occasionally and abstractly, as is often the case today.

While the daily confrontation with life in its many and varied forms had great benefits, it also had drawbacks. One had to confront constantly the other fellow's peculiarities. The city lacked privacy, amenities and room to be together with one's own kind, undisturbed. The walking city with its dirt from wood- and coal-burning ovens and stoves, its stench from horse manure and inadequate sewage and its general overcrowdedness impressed no one as a particularly good place to live. The city lacked the amenities for a peaceful, quiet and pastoral existence.

The city's traffic patterns reflected this deficiency. Even though the walking city was not crowded with people rushing to work and back home, it was crowded with people who for their relaxation went for walks to get away from the physical and mental oppressions of the over-crowded household. These excessive needs for recreational trips are clear symptoms of the basic deficiencies of the walking city, its lack of privacy, its stink and its dirt. It is these trips that signify the walking city's pathology, and at the same time explain why with improved trans-portation people located where they could find greater privacy, clean air and the scent of flowers.

CHAPTER 3

The Tracked City

Before the advent of the railroad it was inconceivable that people should travel beyond comfortable walking distance to meet their day-to-day needs. This was not because the walking city was a place where a person preferred to spend all his time. It was rather a necessary evil to be contended with in earning one's daily bread. Long before the nineteenth century the rich and powerful did maintain second residences beyond the city, such as the castles of Versailles, Windsor, Potsdam and Schoenbrunn. But the commute between these and the primary residence in town was infrequent, and a horse-drawn carriage provided speedy enough transportation. The complete absence of the notion of daily commuting is illustrated by the possibly apocryphal tale of a few enterprising entrepreneurs who tried to obtain a charter for a railroad from Potsdam to Berlin. They told the King that with this new invention he could be in Berlin by eleven in the morning rather than three in the afternoon. To this the King replied, 'And what do I want to do in Berlin at eleven?'

New transportation modes create new spatial patterns, new social relations and new ideas of what constitutes a comfortable travel distance for everyday activities. The nineteenth century witnessed the emergence of a city that was based on quite different spatial, social and economic relations than the walking city that preceded it. This new evolving city we have called the 'tracked city', because its transportation was dominated by vehicles mounted on tracks: railroads and streetcars.

The tracked city, with its jingling streetcars, provided for many a more attractive way of living. Tracked transportation allowed people to escape from the irritating crowdedness of the walking city and to still be involved in the city's economic activities. It made possible the politically and physically separated suburbs and it also provided the means by which the spatially limited walking city was changed into a city of distinct neighborhoods surrounded by suburbs. It stratified the city into separate quarters for the rich, the moderately well-to-do and the poor. In these stratifications, like groups could find special quarters. There could be neighborhoods for intellectuals, the artistically inclined, professionals, civil servants and ethnic minorities. Such areas were not, as in the walking city, restricted to a block or two, but could be large enough to allow the daily contacts of many to be restricted to persons of similar background and life style.

While the tracked city gave some people more choice in their associations, it brought new problems. Now the poor could be isolated in the most undesirable areas, for the tracked city was also the creator of the industrial slum.

In one sense the tracked city evolved out of the walking city as a response to pressures created by the industrial revolution. These pressures were created by the urbanization process, which was the natural concomitant of the industrial revolution. To the extent that some way had to be found to house all the workers around the factory and, failing that, to find ways of transporting them back and forth between home and work place, the tracked city was indeed a response to the industrial revolution. However, the shape of the tracked city was primarily a response to the dirt, noise and pollution of the walking city. It was a response to the need for escape from 'Coketown', to use Mumford's phrase, the final and most horrible form of the walking city.

People throughout history were very conscious of pollution if it occurred on a massive scale. They took active steps to limit it where technically and economically feasible. Thus, in the nineteenth century, because wood- and coal-burning locomotives polluted, the steam railroads, which revolutionized inter-city transportation, were not accepted into the cities as a means of urban transportation. Other means had to be found to provide effective urban transportation for people and goods.

In response to these needs and limitations, the nineteenth century saw the development of many different types of transportation systems. Some were successful, some were not, but basically all fell into two distinct classes. There were the street systems that operated as the term implies on the public streets: the horse-drawn omnibus, the rail-mounted horsecar, the cable car and most important of them all the electric streetcar. Then there were the rapid transit systems that operated on their own right-of-way: the elevated, the underground and the subway.

Historically, the first street system was the omnibus. The Latin origin of the name means 'for all', but the horse-drawn vehicles never quite lived up to their name. The omnibus, a rectangular closed vehicle that could carry between twelve and twenty passengers, was drawn by teams of two and three horses hitched in parallel. The oldest omnibus, or *carosse à cinq sous*, was the brainchild of Blaise Pascal and his associates and made its début in Paris in 1662. After an initial burst of curious interest from the upper classes, the vehicle quickly fell into disuse because it could not attract sufficient fare-paying riders.[1] Apparently most considered walking more economically attractive and nearly as fast.

The omnibus reappeared about 1812 in Bordeaux and about 1827 in Paris. This time it quickly spread to other cities. In 1829, George Shillibeer, the Englishman who had designed the 1827 Paris omnibuses, returned to London determined to introduce it there. On 4 July 1829, the following advertisement appeared in *The British Traveller*:

OMNIBUS

G. Shillibeer, induced by the universal admiration the above vehicle called forth at Paris, has commenced running one upon the Paris mode from Paddington to Bank.

The superiority of the carriage over the ordinary Stage Coaches for comfort and safety must be obvious, all the passengers being Inside, and the Fare charged from Paddington to the Bank being One Shilling, and from Islington to the Bank or Paddington, Sixpence. . . The Proprietor begs to add, that a person of great respectability attends his Vehicle as Conductor; and every possible attention will be paid to the accommodation of Ladies and Children.

Hours of Starting: From Paddington to the Bank at 9, 12, 3, 6, and 8 o'clock; from the Bank to Paddington, at 10, 1, 4, 7, and 9 o'clock.[2]

At the time Shillibeer was introducing the omnibus to London, Abraham Brower in New York began running a stagecoach-like vehicle

---

1. Ellison Hawks, *The Romance of Transportation*, Thomas Y. Crowell Co., New York, 1931, page 113.

2. ibid., page 115.

called an 'accommodation' which seated twelve passengers. To the extent that omnibuses plied the streets of London until nearly the First World War, they can be judged a 'success'. To the extent that they were initiated in many other cities, they can also be judged a 'success'.

In terms of solving the public transportation, or transit, problem these vehicles must be judged a failure. The reasons were much the same as those that plague most modern transit systems. To be acceptable as a public system, the omnibus had to be safe. For practical purposes it had to be impossible to turn it over. To achieve such stability the carriage had to be wide and the wheels far apart. But to limit the team to three horses and still carry a full passenger load the vehicle had to have large wheels. Only such wheels could keep the axle friction to a minimum. Large wheels in turn raised the height of the bus and its center of gravity, which meant that for stability's sake the bus had to be even wider. The end result was a bulky and cumbersome vehicle that was slow and difficult to maneuver, especially in turns and along narrow streets. With four horses it might have been less bulky for the wheel size could have been smaller, but then operating costs would have increased. A smaller vehicle pulled by three horses might also have permitted smaller wheels and less bulk, but then the revenue would have been lower. The omnibus – not unlike today's transit bus – presented a rather precarious balance between what was public acceptable in terms of safety and what was economically feasible in terms of costs and revenues. Or to put it differently, there were few routes on which the omnibus could operate profitably. Basically these routes were restricted to broad avenues in flat terrain where there was considerable traffic throughout the day and not just during rush hours. The omnibus could supply service for shoppers, but not for commuters, and the latter was needed if the bus was to extend the size of the city.

Mounting the bus on rails was the first improvement in an attempt to find a transit system capable of expanding the city. A vehicle that had flanged wheels running on rails was far stabler than a wagon that ran on the cobblestone streets full of potholes. Being inherently stable, streetcars could be narrower than buses and thus maneuver and turn more easily on narrow streets. The much lower friction between wheel and rail, in contrast to wheel and road, meant that the same load could be pulled by less power. Most horse-drawn streetcars carried about eighteen to twenty passengers, just as the omnibuses, but the power was supplied by one horse rather than three. The horsecars could also operate on hills and, if need be, two horses could pull them. With lower friction and smoother road surfaces, the power needed to start up the streetcar, unlike the omnibus, did not differ greatly from the power needed to keep it moving. Thus, the wheels on the horsecar could be much smaller than those of the omnibus. This contributed to the safety of the car by lowering its center of gravity, and to the convenience of the passengers by reducing the number of steps that had to be climbed.

Even with all these advantages, the street railways had a serious handicap. Tracks had to be laid before operations could begin. When demand for service shifted, the routes could not be changed. But even this cloud had its silver lining. When streetcar lines showed no profit, they were not as quickly abandoned as bus lines, especially during the first years of operation. This gave the potential customers time to adapt their behavior patterns to the new transportation system.

The first effective urban street-railway transportation system was started in New York City in 1852. Within the next four years similar systems appeared in Philadelphia and Boston. In England, the first tracks for street railways were laid at Birkenhead in 1860, London in 1861, and in the Potteries (North Staffordshire) in 1863.[3] During the following decade, horse-drawn streetcars appeared in nearly all major cities.

Transit commuting began with the horsecar, but only on a very limited basis, for the horse was an inadequate power source upon which to expand cities. In addition to average speeds of only four to six miles an hour, hardly faster than walking, horse power was expensive. While the drivers would work an 'honest' ten to twelve hour day, the horses called it quits after four or five hours. Even with these hours, the horses lasted only a few years; after that they had to be sold for lighter service – cheaply. Furthermore horses, being animals and not machines, became sick and were subject to epidemics. An especially bad one occurred in 1872 when a respiratory disease killed over 2,250 horses in Philadelphia and affected over 18,000 in New York.[4] It is hardly

3. Emile Garcke, 'Tramway', *Encyclopedia Britannica*, eleventh edn, Vol. XXVII, 1911, page 159.

4. George Smerk, *Urban Transportation: The Federal Role*, Univ. of Indiana Press, Bloomington, 1965.

astonishing that streetcar operators looked for a cheaper and more reliable power source than the horse.

Steam was the obvious candidate. Unfortunately for street-railway use, steam had two drawbacks. One was pollution. A steam-powered streetcar spewed its soot over pedestrians and others on the street and its noise frightened the horses. The other was the need to build up a head of steam to move the driving piston from its starting position. This made steam locomotives ill-suited for frequent starts and stops – the very essence of a streetcar system. Steam-powered cable car systems met both these objectives. Here a steam engine pulled cables that ran under the streetcar tracks. The streetcar had a long fork which hung from the car and passed through a slot in the street and gripped the cable which then propelled the car. The car was stopped by releasing the cable grip and applying the brakes. The first steam-powered cable car line was built in San Francisco in 1873.[5] During the 1880s, other systems were built in England and America. The most extensive was Chicago's, with 86 miles of track and 469 grip cars.[6] The cable car never became a great success because of its high initial cost and questionable reliability. A better solution was still needed, and a better solution was soon discovered in the electrically powered streetcar, the trolley.[7]

By the late 1880s technology had advanced sufficiently to make electric power a realistic alternative to the tired horse and the unreliable cable. The first feasible electric streetcar system was built in Richmond, Virginia, and was a success from the day it opened in 1888. Richmond's

5. Edward Throm (ed.), *Popular Mechanics' Picture History of American Transportation*, Simon & Schuster, New York, 1952, page 103.

6. ibid., page 103.

7. In engineering parlance a trolley is the grooved metalic pulley which travels along, and receives current from, an overhead electric wire. Because the early U.S. electric streetcars used such a device they became known as 'trolleys', probably in part to distinguish them from the horse-drawn streetcars, the horsecars. In Britain the horse-drawn and electric streetcars were both known as 'trams' and the word 'trolley' as applied to a public transport vehicle came into use only later when people desired to distinguish between the electric powered bus and the motor bus. We use the word 'trolley' to speak of electric streetcars and the words 'trolley bus' to speak of electric buses operating on overhead wires.

electrics were larger than horsecars, could travel at speeds of ten to twelve miles an hour, and would work a human day. With this successful demonstration the rush was on. All over the world, city after city converted its horsecar tracks to electric power, and, what was far more important, built new streetcar lines. Within a decade the effective size of many cities had been extended from a radius of two and one-half miles to about six miles. In America, between 1890 and 1902, electric streetcar mileage jumped from 1,200 to 21,900 while horsecar trackage declined from 5,500 to barely 250 miles.[8] It was truly a period of expanding urban transportation.

Even though trolleys could travel at 12 miles per hour and faster, they were often not able to do so. Then, as now, the inner city streets were crowded, traffic moved at a crawl and often got badly snarled. Under these conditions streetcars, however powered, could not maintain a reliable schedule. There were either several in a row or none at all. Especially in the large cities with over a million population and mammoth traffic jams, streetcars were not the full answer. Still more reliable, faster transportation was needed.

The answer seemed to be lightweight railroads that had their own tracks not on the street, but above or below it, the elevated and the underground. Unfortunately, with steam the primary motive power, neither elevated nor subway were really acceptable. Both polluted the rider and the neighborhood. In addition, the columns that supported the tracks of the elevated interfered with the street traffic below.

To minimize pollution many schemes were proposed. In London, Sir John Fowler worked on a steam engine which could be charged at both ends of the subway line with water and steam at high pressure so that steam generation and fire were not needed while the train was en route. Since Fowler was the chief engineer of London's Metropolitan Line this scheme was part of the proposal that won the 1854 charter for building the line, the world's first subway. The engine, which was known as 'Fowler's Ghost', never really worked, and when the line

8. John F. Stover, *The Life and Decline of the American Railroad*, Oxford University Press, New York, 1970, page 129.

9. John R. Day, *The Story of London's Underground*, London Transport, London, 1969, pages 9–12.

opened in 1863 normally fired engine systems were used.[9] These engines worked, but there were outcries from the riding public about poor ventilation. At one station a fan was provided; at others the glass was removed from the windows. Later, in 1871–2, to improve ventilation further blowholes were bored through the roof of the tunnels to the road above. But this created new problems. As the trains passed, the air, steam, smoke and soot rushed from the holes below and scared the horses above.[10]

The first elevated was built in New York in 1868. Here the motive power was supplied by stationary steam engines that pulled a wire cable. When the line reached from Greenwich Street to 30th Street the stationary steam engines could no longer produce the power that was needed to operate the cable. To keep the system working, squat, undersized steam engines were substituted for the cables. With these little polluters the elevated became a stunning success in New York. They opened up Manhattan Island for settlement north of Midtown. In 1878 there were elevated lines running up and down the Island along 2nd, 3rd, 6th and 9th Avenues.[11] Still, no one wanted to live on a street with an el if it could be avoided. New York's housing illustrates this point. Along the four avenues tenements were built while one-family brown-stones graced the crosstown streets that were in easy walking distance of the els.

Neither elevated nor subways found wide acceptance prior to the introduction of electric-powered trains. The Metropolitan and District Lines in London, the Mersey Railway in Liverpool and the Stadtbahn in Vienna were the only subway systems that were built with steam traction, and only a fourth of the mileage of the Vienna system was in tunnels. In addition to New York, elevated lines with steam traction were built in Berlin, Brooklyn and Chicago. Except in Berlin, these lines were built mainly in areas which were not yet settled. In Berlin the elevated, the Stadtbahn, did not operate over streets but had its right-of-way on top of embankments.

When electric traction became a reality during the 1890s a boom in subway building began. In 1896 Budapest opened its system, the first on the European continent, and two years later Boston put the first

10. ibid., page 15.

11. Edward Robb Ellis, *The Epic of New York City: A Narrative History from 1524 to the Present*, Coward-McCann, Inc., New York, 1966, page 340.

American subway system into service. This trend which began before the turn of the century, has continued and is in fact accelerating (see Figure 1). At present more cities are building new systems than at any previous time, and old systems, including London and New York, are still adding lines.

While most types of transportation reach their maturity rather quickly, the subways have grown more consistently and over a longer period of time than any other transportation mode that came into being

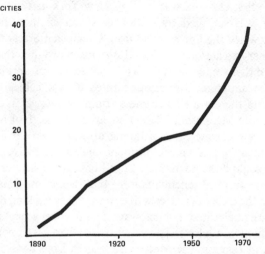

NUMBER OF CITIES

Fig. 1. *Rapid transit, underground and surface railways: number of cities with operating systems* (*data from* Jane's World Railways; *711–726*)

since the industrial revolution. The subway system apparently not only met a real need in the past, but, is also meeting a need in the present.

The tracked city that evolved with these new means of transportation was not just an oversized walking city. It was not the walking city with greater distances between activities. On the contrary, it was a quite differently organized and shaped city that radically altered land-use and life-style patterns. The forms and patterns of the tracked city are the responses to the desires to escape pollution and the daily irritations that are part and parcel of the walking city. It all began with the industrial revolution and the railroads. Those two forces combined to penetrate and transform the old cities, market towns and trading centers. Both were repelled at the gates of the old city and with seemingly diabolic revenge began to transform the cities from their peripheries.

When the early railroads were first chartered and built, they were not permitted to enter or traverse the populated areas. This was particularly true of the national capitals of Europe, which were major urban centers well before the railroad age. The railroads ended at what were then the outskirts of the city, and here the lines built their terminals.[12] As a result, most old major cities do not have one main railroad station but nearly as many terminals as lines that serve the city, to the everlasting chagrin of those who just pass through the city.

The same general pattern for locating railroads also occurred in the smaller cities. Here too the railroads were kept out of the built-up areas. Rare indeed is the exception, but the most notable is Cologne, where the main railroad station is next to the medieval cathedral.

Environmental factors, and not just cost considerations, kept the railroads at the outskirts of the cities. This is apparent from local ordinances in New York. The first railroad in New York City was the New York and Harlem, which opened in 1832. The city terminus was then at City Hall and Chambers Street, well within the built-up area. From there the railroad cars, which were pulled by mules and horses, proceeded up Manhattan Island. In 1839, however, steam locomotives replaced the animals. The pine-burning engines with their sparks, smoke and general din immediately led to public indignation which reached its height when a boiler exploded at 14th Street. The city then passed an ordinance which banned steam locomotives from the populated part of the Island. For the next few years single railroad coaches drawn by horses operated between the in-city terminal and the depot on the edge of town, where the cars were coupled up into trains to be hauled by steam engines further up the Island.[13]

The railroads were not all that was stopped at the city's edge: industry, too, found this an impenetrable barrier. Then as now the location

12. The one exception appears to be the Stadtbahn in Berlin, but this road was not built until the 1870s and then primarily as an elevated for intra-urban traffic, though suburban and long-distance trains shared the same right-of-way atop the embankment.

13. Susan E. Lyman, *The Story of New York: An Informal History of the City*, Crown Publishers, New York, 1965, pages 132–3.

of industry depended on three basic factors: vacant land, available labor, and a transportation system capable of bringing raw materials and distributing finished products. The steam railroad made it possible for industrial plants to shift from the mouth of the coal mines, where labor was scarce, to any locale to which coal could be economically transported. The railroads permitted industry to locate close to the market towns and trading centers or at least at the edge of these cities. Here vacant land along the railroad tracks was available for building factories, and workers could walk from the inner city to the industrial plants. In those locations where industry preceded the railroad, there was a tendency to run the new tracks as close to the plants as possible to generate freight revenue.

Because they needed open land, industry and rails tended to move out from the city; but because they also needed distribution and access to labor and passengers, they tended to move as close to the built-up area as possible. The result was that in the mid-1800s distinct railroad yards and manufacturing belts began to surround the pre-railroad city.

Where there were no social or political constraints on industrial locations, as in the United States, the belt surrounded the entire city, and under all wind conditions the soot of its smoke stacks would engulf the city. Where industry lacked this freedom, as in Europe's national capitals and commercial cities, the belt was generally restricted to the city's leeward side. Since industry and rail never required all the vacant land they polluted with soot and noise, or always blighted more land than they occupied, the question of usage for this blighted land arose. The answer was 'perfectly' simple. The land was 'ideal' for housing the unskilled rural and immigrant work force that streamed into the city to satisfy the labor demands of rail and industry.

With industry and rail, cities now received distinct new housing sections built to be slums. Poor housing was not an invention of the mid 1800s, but poor housing now took a different form. Previously most city housing had been built to supply quarters for the owner's family, his business and those who worked for him. Later such housing might convert to slum housing but it was not built for that purpose. Prior to the 1830s housing built just for the unskilled labor force, for the city's poor, was rare indeed. There were exceptions, such as the Fuggerei in Augsburg. But with the industrial revolution and the rails, nearly every city received tenement housing in which the builder-owners never planned to live.

The tenements were simply horrible. Families were crowded together with a minimum of privacy, air and light. According to Lewis Mumford, conditions of life in the American tenement were much worse than they had been in the primitive farmhouses of the colonial period.[14] New York's so-called 'dumbbell' tenements were in some respects the worst of all, despite their winning first prize in a model tenement design competition. Here, on lots 25 feet wide and 100 feet deep, houses were erected which were 25 by 90 feet. This left a 10-foot backyard for hanging out the wash – and air. The buildings were five to seven stories high with four apartments and two water closets on each floor. Each apartment had three rooms: one opened on the street or on the tiny backyard, two had tiny windows that opened on an airshaft 4 feet wide and 50 to 60 feet long. These airshafts gave the floor plan a dumbbell shape and hence the name for the tenements. The shafts were much too small to let any air into the backrooms. Air could not circulate in the shafts but hung heavy and foul. It is said that these shafts were often used for refuse, which hardly helped the quality of air. These were the living quarters of people who, because they had no access to transportation, had to live where they could walk to their ten- or twelve-hour work day without too great a loss of time and energy.

Where the belt surrounded the entire city, no one could consider the city a desirable place to live. Where the belt was only on the leeward side, which in the northern hemisphere means the east side of town, the west side became the quarters of the affluent while the industrial workers were relegated to the city's east side, as illustrated by London and Berlin. In general, cities grew faster at their fringes than at their core from the advent of the belt (1830–50) and have lost population at the core since 1860.

With the arrival of the electric streetcars, the trolleys, both the fully and partially belted cities began to spread in territory, but somewhat differently. When the partially belted city began to expand, the affluent middle and upper classes moved further towards the west. This was

14. Lewis B. Mumford, *Sticks and Stones: A Study of American Architecture and Civilization*, second edn, Dover Publications, Inc., New York, 1955, page 109.

not so much a headlong flight from the stench of the city to the lee, which they could only rarely smell, but because they needed more land for their increasing numbers. Meanwhile, the working and lower-middle classes spread beyond the belt towards the east, north and south. Where the belt more completely encircled the city, all but the poor fled beyond the belt – this was a flight, not just a spreading due to the city's population growth. In these cities a person's status had little to do with the direction of his flight, but in all cases the distance a person moved from the city core was directly related to his affluence. The unskilled stayed in the slums, where they could walk to work. The skilled and lower-middle classes tended to go beyond the belt as far out as crosstown transportation would permit. This provided relatively easy access to several work locations which in turn accommodated the needs of households with several workers. A middle-class family, with a single worker who had a steady place of employment, could afford to go further out. A radial streetcar line that brought the worker to his place of employment was all the transportation necessary. Finally, the affluent who wanted to bring up their families away from the clatter of the city moved to the quiet country village, 'the suburbs', which could be reached only by railroad. Since the latter group could control their hours of work, limited and infrequent transportation was no insurmountable handicap to the enjoyment of suburban spaciousness.

The middle-class families' desire to jump the belt for a cleaner, more livable environment created, particularly in the United States, the opportunity for land speculators to make sizable profits by combining trolley operations with real-estate developments. The device was simple. A trolley line, charging low fares, was built beyond the city to marginal land, owned by the speculators. This land was then subdivided into building lots. The result was a manifold increase in the value of these real-estate holdings, which more than made up for operating trolley lines that were at best barely profitable. This connection between real-estate profits and transit availability was thoroughly understood by U.S. land speculators from coast to coast.

Like any undertaking where sizable speculative profits can be realized quickly, political chicanery and underhanded financial dealings were common. Indeed, the municipal scandals at the turn of the century uncovered by Lincoln Steffens, the muckraker, were mainly about transit dealings. Political chicanery arose largely because the transit lines needed to operate on the public right-of-ways, or required the power of eminent domain to acquire their own right-of-way. To gain this access, charters and franchise privileges had to be secured from state and local government officials. Inevitably competitors sought and found public officials who for a slice of the pie became favorably disposed towards their application. Even without corruption, the need for franchises led to a publicly fostered overproliferation of transit lines, since the sale of every new franchise brought additional revenues to the public treasury. It was common for lines to run on parallel streets and to serve the same small segment of the urban transit market.

One might assume that with the arrival of the railroads the affluent began to move to the quiet country villages from where they could commute by rail to the city. This, however, was only rarely the case. The extensive moves began only with the development of urban transit systems. In the suburbs a man could locate his home within easy walking distance of the railroad station, but in the city he had to take what was given. If the walk from the city terminal to work was too far, commuting was too cumbersome as a daily activity. But with the arrival of crosstown transit commuting became practical, and the affluent started to migrate to the railroad suburbs.

As people moved beyond the belt to the streetcar and railroad developments, additional inner city land became available for offices and commercial establishments. This resulted in a commercial building boom. The introduction of elevators around 1870 made taller buildings possible and further spurred the inner city construction boom. The new buildings were most apt to be near the railroad stations where the trains departed for the most affluent suburbs. For as every cynical management consultant knows, the boss's residence is a most vital, if rarely voiced, factor in plant location. His commute must be easy.

If this maxim is true, why didn't the flight of industry to the suburbs begin with the tracked city? If the business was a manufacturing plant with billowing smoke stacks, the proprietor's wife, for one, did not want to live near it. She wanted a clean, not a sooty, house. If the business was warehousing, wholesaling or distribution, it required that goods be shipped to various places in the local urban area. In the tracked city this was done by horse-drawn wagons, a terribly costly and cumbersome way to move large quantities of goods. The economics of business simply required that shipping distances be kept to a minimum. A move to the suburbs would have bankrupted too many businesses. Some attempts were made to utilize trolleys and rapid transit for local freight service. However, this was not sufficient, since transshipments by horse-drawn wagon were still needed. The hauling of mail between post offices was one of the few exceptions where the trolleys and rapid transit lines proved to be effective shipping modes.

The tracked city's principal influence was on the spatial arrangements between workplace and home. In the walking city neither people nor goods could move easily. In the tracked city people could move faster and with greater ease, but goods could not. Thus the tracked city had to concentrate all activities that involved the movement of goods, but could fan out the activities that involved only the movement of people. People no longer had to live near their workplaces, but could find congenial locations for their residences. On the other hand the place of work was determined by the industry or the activity it served. Not even the bosses could move it freely, as would be the case in the rubber city.

The immobility of goods and the economically stratified mobility of the population were also reflected in the structure of the tracked city's neighborhoods and suburbs.

From the start the residential suburbs attracted not only the affluent who lived there and worked in the city, but also local service and retailing businesses that served the community. Each suburb had its bakers, grocers, school teachers, firemen, shoemakers, street-sweepers, servants, gardeners and general laborers who lived and worked within the suburb. Some of these people were the natives, whose families lived in the village long before it became a suburb. In contrast to the suburbs of the rubber city, the suburbs of the tracked city were not restricted to one income group but had within their corporate limits people of all income classes, though not to the same extent as in the central city. While there was segregation in the tracked metropolis – specifically most of the poor were isolated from all the others – none of the middle and upper classes lived in the antiseptically isolated communities of modern suburbia.

When society was stratified by race and ethnic background, as in America, the tracked city also saw the development of the urban Negro ghetto and ethnic neighborhoods. Other groups, too – the artist colonies and the university sections – began to coalesce in special neighborhoods. Nevertheless, these territorial segregation patterns are but subvariations within the basic economic stratifications. Poor and lace-curtain Irish did not live in the same neighborhood, nor poor and well-to-do blacks in the same part of Harlem.

At the time of the tracked city the suburbs were solidly anchored to the rails. If there was no track to the city, a suburb could not arise. Thus the tracked metropolis could not spread in a set of concentric belts or rings around the core of the city as many models seem to indicate. This pattern held only as far out as there was crosstown transportation. Beyond this area, the metropolis did not expand in rings, but along the streetcar and railroad lines that ran radially out of the city. This gave the tracked metropolis a starshaped pattern, most obvious in the completely belted cities such as Chicago, Philadelphia/Camden and Detroit. It is less pronounced in the partially belted cities such as London and Berlin. In the belted cities the only possible growth was to jump the belt along the same corridor that industry used. The suburbs along these corridors had to be further from the center of the city than those along corridors with little or no industry. Then, too, if no industrial belt surrounded the 'better' part of the city, there was less pressure to move to distant suburbs. The residential areas closer to the city were sufficiently clean and spacious to serve the needs of the most affluent, and with streetcars and underground they had more frequent transportation service than the railroad suburbs.

The tighter the industrial belt surrounded the old walking city, the more the tracked city burst forth in a star pattern with extremely long commute lines. But this was not the end of the belt's influence. With the coming of the truck and the car the points of the star become the Achilles' heel of the rubber city.

CHAPTER 4

The Rubber City

In our romanticizing the past we tend to regard the city around the beginning of the century, in the years before and after the First World War, as a sort of ideal. With clanging streetcars, shaded residential streets and Sunday excursions, everything appeared to be at peace and in balance. Strange as it may seem, as far as transportation is concerned, it is possible that for one short moment this balance actually did exist for the using public. For it is a fact that during these years city traffic improved steadily, and there was a marked reduction of congestion in the heart of the city.

The streetcar did not create this balance. Too much was wrong with it. Though streetcars increased the size of the city by increasing the areas devoted to residential neighborhoods, they had little effect on the size of the commercial and industrial quarters. Freight within the city was still carried by horse-drawn dray. The inability of the streetcars to improve freight transportation was not their only drawback. With streetcars people could only travel where the streetcars went. If one didn't want to go where they went, one had no transportation. While the streetcars went up and down the avenues and along the main arterials, this was all the transportation they furnished. Since streetcars went where most wanted to go, they were good for massing people, getting them to work, to shopping and the main amusement attractions. But for those who wanted to go along the routes where few traveled, streetcars at best required numerous transfers, were cumbersome, terribly slow and most likely non-existent. Thus for visiting friends, for fellows to date the girls from the office rather than the one next door, or for getting to quiet spots in the country, streetcar transportation was rarely the solution.

The rich had a solution. They used private horse-drawn carriages. During the nineteenth century, ever newer, safer and more comfortable carriages were built, and increasingly more private carriages and carriages-for-hire were seen on city streets. But this form of transportation was much too expensive for the average citizen. Fortunately, just when urban transportation approached the unbearable, a number of new systems in addition to the streetcars made their appearance and created the momentary euphoria which we remember so fondly.

First there was the bicycle. The bicycle developed slowly from the early-nineteenth-century hobby horse, to the high 'ordinary' bicycle with its large oversized front wheel and small rear wheel of the 1870s and 1880s, to the safety bicycle with pneumatic tires which came into vogue around 1890, and which is substantially the bicycle as we know it today. The early bicycles were strictly for sport and recreation. This was particularly true of the 'ordinary', with its enormous front wheel, five feet or more in diameter. The rider sat on top of this wheel and had his head eight to nine feet above the ground. Considerable agility was required to ride these monstrosities, and a fall was quite a bounce. Far less skill was needed to ride the safety bikes. Not only the highly athletic but the clumsy as well as the dainty could enjoy the new-found freedom they offered. By the turn of the century bicycle riding had advanced from a pastime to a convenient means of locomotion for everyday use – level terrain and weather permitting.

The bicycle was the first form of private transportation within the financial means of the average citizen. It gave those of modest income, who physically could ride them, access when they wanted it to many places that could not be reached by streetcar or on the streetcar's schedule. From the point of view of transportation, the bicycle is the true forerunner of the private mass-produced automobile. Like the forerunners they were, bicycle riders and bicycle clubs were also the first agitators for better roads, an agitation that, under the influence of the automobile would be elevated to a crescendo.

Like the bicycle, the automobile had its beginning in the early nineteenth century, when the first steam-propelled vehicles were built. Here solid fuels were burned to generate steam, which then propelled the vehicle. This double conversion of energy was rather inefficient and required engines of considerable size and weight. Since these vehicles were far too large for the available roads, steam locomotion went nowhere until it was placed on tracks. To make quite sure that such oversized machines would stay off the highways, the British House of Commons enacted, in the 1860s, Locomotives on Highway Acts, which required three operators on each vehicle, a person in front of the vehicle waving a red flag, and a maximum speed of four miles an hour. To make motorized highway transportation feasible, a much smaller, lighter and more efficient engine was needed. This was the gasoline-powered internal-combustion engine. By the 1880s the first gasoline-powered cars were built on the Continent, and finally in 1896 the House of Commons repealed the prohibitive clauses of the Locomotives on Highway Acts.

Up to the late 1890s, the development was primarily European. After that Americans too began to build cars. Finally, in 1908, Henry Ford produced a relatively inexpensive, rugged, all-purpose car, the Model T Ford, which sold for $825 while most other cars were still priced above $1,500. This significant breakthrough made Ford's car a major factor in converting the automobile from a sporty showpiece into a practical mode of transportation. Another, and at least equally important, factor was the invention of the electric starter by Charles Kettering. The electric starter replaced the crank and enlarged the potential driving population beyond the highly muscular. How important this invention was can be seen by the speed of its adoption and its effect on automobile production. Invented in 1911, electric starters were first offered commercially on the 1912 Cadillac and by 1916 on over 90 per cent of all American-produced cars. Meanwhile U.S. car production jumped between 1912 and 1916 by 330 per cent from 356,000 to 1,525,000 cars per year.

The early automobile presented a distinct improvement for urban transportation. It was more economical to own and operate than a horse-drawn carriage, but was still not within the financial range of the average wage earner. Since it could carry passengers, it was more sociable than the bicycle. This was particularly important, as the early automobile, like the bicycle, was a supplementary mode of transportation, not a vehicle for meeting basic urban transportation needs. The early auto, again like the bicycle, was mainly used for recreation. It was a means to escape the crowded and dirty city for an outing into the open country. As long as cars were bought as replacements for horse-drawn carriages, they did not contribute to the congestion of the city. In fact they relieved the congestion, because cars required less street space than horse and carriage combinations. On unpaved roads cars were noisier than horses, but on pavement their noise was different, though not worse than the clanging of hoofs. In spite of their exhaust fumes, cars did not increase the city's air pollution and dirt. Cars create less stink and irritation than horses, who leave their fly-attracting calling cards everywhere.

Although the bicycle and the early automobile dramatically improved accessibility, they had only minimal effect on urban congestion. Here three quite different systems showed their mettle. First, there were the rapid transit systems: the subways and the elevated. These intra-urban railroads were restricted to the largest of the large cities and where they existed they offered not only faster transportation, but substantial relief to street crowding.

Another major factor in relieving the crowded streets was the introduction of the motorized truck. This began around 1905. For a time at least, the increased efficiency of the electric- and gasoline-powered trucks far outstripped the continued growth of the cities. It may sound incongruous to us, where we curse today's trucks for obstructing traffic, but in the early days of motorized transportation the truck did relieve traffic. Trucks require far less street space to move a ton than a horse-drawn dray, and are far more maneuverable. Just compare the ease with which even a large trailer truck can be backed into a loading dock to the shouting, cussing and shoving that is associated with getting a cumbersome team of horses to back up a foot or two.

Simultaneously with the truck, buses were introduced into the urban scene. The first buses operated in London in 1904 and in Paris and New York during the following year. These early buses usually replaced horse-drawn omnibuses and, as in New York, were the transit system of the more affluent. Here the first buses operated along Fifth Avenue, the city's best shopping and residential street. These buses guaranteed each rider a seat and charged twice the fare of the paralleling streetcars and subways.

The third invention that relieved inner city traffic was the telephone. With this marvel, short messages can be passed from counting house to counting house without requiring the services of a runner or a boy on a bicycle. Without leaving their offices, people can make agreements to meet at an appointed place and time, rather than taking a walk at noon or going to the club or pub in the vain hope of running into one another. The telephone obsoleted to some extent one very basic function of the city, the common meeting place, the agora, where everyone who is anyone meets every other anyone. By its very nature, the traffic necessary to mass people creates congestion and traffic jams. Thus the telephone, which in the long run may have increased overall traffic by speeding up the tempo of business, did in the beginning reduce precisely that aspect of traffic most productive of annoyance and user criticism – traffic congestion.

The urban transportation balance of the early twentieth century was short lived – especially in the United States – and was at best a precarious one. In the main the balance had been created by the rise of private transportation which counterbalanced the earlier rise of public transportation, but this was also the force that would destroy it. For cars and trucks continued to grow while in too many cities public transportation languished.

Transit languished in U.S. cities for many reasons. Some arose from the sharp financial dealing under which many streetcar lines were chartered, others because transit was chartered in a piecemeal fashion, line by line, rather than as one city-wide system. But if these were the only problems the stagnation would not have been so widespread. Mergers and reorganizations should have been sufficient to rehabilitate transit in most cities. These, however, were never sufficient, since private companies could not achieve the profits, the return on investment, needed to attract capital. The original franchise holders had set the fares too low to derive maximum or even reasonable profits from transit operations. They did this because their profits resulted from the increased land value transit generated. To cause these real-estate appreciations, the transit system had to attract significant ridership volumes, and this required low fares. As long as real-estate profits could be realized by building and subsidizing transit lines, there was an impetus for the private sector to provide the needed subsidies and build, operate and even refurbish transit lines.

But once the real-estate had been developed and sold, the developers had no desire to subsidize the fares and sought fare increases. In general, this occurred during or right after the First World War, a period of generally rising labor costs and prices. Fare increases were granted, but they were rarely as large as the transit operators desired.

Had the fares been hiked to the extent necessary to make the lines truly profitable ventures, the ridership would have dropped so drastically that the spatial arrangement of the urban area, created by the transit systems, would have been socially and economically unable to function. To an urban society the value of transit lines stems precisely from their ability to carry large volumes of traffic through spatial arrangements that are considerably larger than those of the walking city. Thus governmental authorities were pressured by residents, employers and retailers alike not to grant the steep fare increases needed by the private operators to generate profit margins large enough to attract new capital in the open market. Most of the expansion of urban transit lines that occurred during the inter-war years happened either because there was still vacant land that could be developed through instituting transit service, or because congestion relief in the built-up areas required increased transit service. In the latter case, public funds or credits invariably furnished most, if not all, the required capital.

While transit languished due to its economic unattractiveness, the expansion of automobile ownership and usage continued unabated through the private profit impetus of the automobile companies and their suppliers. With the destruction of the balance new urban growth patterns developed which in time changed the well-defined built-up city surrounded by agricultural land into metropolitan regions whose outer limits no one is sure of. Both trucks and cars contributed to this transformation, though their effects were quite different, since different social and economic forces spurred the two modes.

The truck arose from a basic deficiency in urban transportation. Not so the car. Here the growth was dictated by rural, intercity and small-town needs rather than the needs of the large urban centers. The automobile, while invented in the city and used there as a rich man's toy, grew to prominence as a mature everyday transportation mode in rural areas and from there invaded the city and transformed it. In this context, the history of automobile transportation suddenly makes sense. It explains why Europe's invention had its earliest and most explosive growth as a transportation system in North America. It explains why the United Kingdom and the rest of Europe are still lagging behind the United States in auto ownership (see Figure 2), and finally it helps us to see what is needed to free our present society from becoming completely engulfed by automobile traffic jams. With this premise, we can explain the growth of auto travel on the basis of economic and human needs and without reference to such popular non-explanatory explanations as, 'the American love affair with the automobile', or 'the automobile as a status symbol'. In the U.S. today there are over 430 cars for every 1,000 population, and the ratio is still growing. This means the U.S. has more

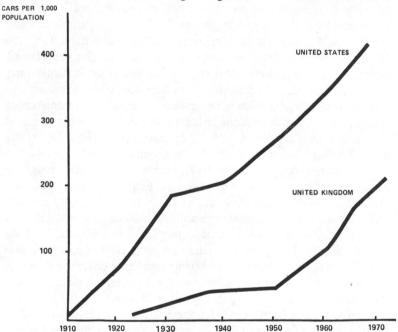

Fig. 2 *Automobile ownership (data from official government publications)*

cars than households, more cars than workers in the labor force, and spends 25 cents of every retail dollar on new and used vehicles, accessories and gasoline. Does any serious student of the rationality of man believe that a country could be engulfed to such extent by a love affair or a status symbol? The automobile grew in answer to real economic and human needs, and it grew so much faster in America than elsewhere, because in America the needs were greatest.

Before Ford and Kettering, the United States had by far the poorest rural and intercity transportation system of all the advanced industrialized nations. In those days in the United States, as in Europe, rural and intercity transportation was by rail and horse-drawn wagon. But there the resemblance ends. In Europe, most railroads operated as regional and national transportation systems, with main and branch lines that tried to meet the social, economic and administrative travel patterns of an area. Train schedules were devised to permit relatively convenient transfer on journeys that involved more than one train ride, since it was to the economic benefit of the railroads to increase system-wide ridership. By contrast, in America the railroads were private companies which had charters, but not necessarily exclusive charters, to operate between two or more cities. No railroad company had exclusive rights to serve a region or an area. As a result, rail lines were not laid out to serve a region, but to connect the two terminal cities. If additional freight and passengers could be picked up along the line, so much the better, but that was the extent of the railroads' concern for these freight shippers and passengers. The train schedules reflected the same philosophy. Each railroad tried to maximize its profits by getting the greatest share of the market rather than by serving the transportation needs of the communities it passed through. Interline and off-hour travelers were served if it was profitable to do so, otherwise they might as well wait until the railroad was good and ready to run a train. This policy makes a lot of sense from the short-term interest of each railroad. It is much easier to steal the other line's passengers than to develop slowly and painstakingly new markets through branch lines or to give frequent service through extra trains. But the long-term effects were equally obvious. Rail travel in the U.S. never became as popular as in Europe. Even in their heydays around 1920, the U.S. railroads on a per capita basis carried only a third of the passengers of the British and German railroads, or a fifth of the passengers of the Swiss system.

The implications of this poor rail service for the business traveler are described beautifully by Fred Allen, the great radio comedian of the 1930s and 40s. Allen worked in his younger years as a vaudeville actor on a circuit that served forty to fifty theaters in eight midwestern states. This is his tale of woe:

The cities and towns of the network of the eight states could seldom be reached by any one railroad. To go from Chicago to the various theaters where he had been booked, the actor traveled on the New York Central,

Chicago and Alton, Santa Fe, Wabash, Union Pacific, Big Four, Chicago and Burlington, Chicago, Milwaukee, and St Paul, and perhaps one or two other railroads. There never seemed to be a direct way the actor could go from one date to another without changing trains once or twice during the night and spending endless hours at abandoned junctions waiting for connecting trains. One trip always annoyed me. Terre Haute and Evansville, both in Indiana, were a split week. The acts playing the Hippodrome Theater in Terre Haute for the first three days went to the Grand Theater in Evansville for the last three. If it had been possible to go directly from one town to the other, the trip could have been made in three hours. It took the actor eight hours. Finishing at Terre Haute, they would leave there on the midnight train. After riding for an hour, they had to get off at some small town and wait four hours for a train to pick them up to ride the remaining two hours to Evansville. Most of the railroad stations were deserted at night. When the actor's trunk was thrown off the train, he had to put it on a truck, pull the truck to the baggage car on the next train, and help the baggageman load it if he wanted to assure the arrival of his wardrobe and his props at the theater the next day. In the Middle West during the winter months the snow-storms were frequent and severe, trains were late, the baggage was lost, but neither rain, sleet, hail, snow, lack of sleep, nor empty stomachs kept the Western Vaudeville acts from making contractual rounds. The show must go on. Through the years, I have spent a hundred nights curled up in the dark, freezing railroad stations in the Kokomos, the Kenoshas, and the Kankakees, waiting for the Big Four, the Wabash, or C&A trains to pick me up and whisk me to the Danvilles, the Davenports, and the Decaturs. Most of the actors playing the Western Vaudeville theaters looked as though they hadn't been to sleep for many months. They looked that way because they hadn't.[1]

It is no wonder that travelers deserted the rails as soon as they could for cars that were reliable and for highways that were not mud roads.

Prior to 1920, half of all Americans lived in what the U.S. Bureau of the Census so charmingly calls 'rural territory', that is, in towns with less than 2,500 population or in the open country. As late as 1940, half of all Americans lived in cities and towns of less than 10,000 population or in the open country. The rails never really served the local transportation needs of these people, for it was the rare exception rather than

1. Fred Allen, *Much Ado About Me*, an Atlantic Monthly Press Book, Little, Brown & Company, Boston, Toronto, 1956, pages 186–7.

the rule if one railroad covered the trade territory of any one area. From a glance at the map it may look as if the cities and towns at least in the eastern half of the country were well served by railroads, when, in fact, they were not, as a perusal of old railroad schedules shows.

There is a small town in Ohio, which its 1830 settlers called New Washington, apparently in the hope of greater things to come. By 1916 the village had a population of about 900, and was the trading center for the surrounding three townships where an additional 3,000 persons lived. New Washington had two railroads, the Ohio Northern, running east–west from Akron to Delphos, Ohio, and the Pennsylvania's Pittsburgh to Toledo line, which ran through the town from the southeast to the northwest. With two railroads, New Washington had two depots one half mile apart. So if you thought you could change in New Washington from the Ohio Northern to the Pennsylvania or vice versa, dear passenger, you had to carry your bag a long half mile. Naturally, since the lines crossed, the depots could have been at the crossings. The Ohio Northern's was, but the Pennsylvania's was not. People had trouble transferring, but freight cars were regularly switched from one line to the other.

New Washington is in Crawford County, fourteen miles from the county seat, Bucyrus. Bucyrus had the service of several lines. There was the Pittsburgh to Chicago mainline of the Pennsylvania, the Pennsylvania's Sandusky to Columbus line, and finally the New York Central's Toledo to Columbus line. There was no direct line from New Washington to Bucyrus. From the map one could conclude that the best train route would be the Ohio Northern to Chatfield and from there by the Pennsylvania's Sandusky to Columbus branch to Bucyrus. This connection, however, made the trip an all-day affair. Connections were better if one took the Pennsylvania all the way. One could leave New Washington at 7:49 A.M., go to Carrothers – an unincorporated village which is as hard to find in nature as to locate on the map – wait for one hour and eighteen minutes and arrive in Bucyrus by 9:46 A.M. To return to New Washington the same day one had to hurry, for the last connection for New Washington left at 10:02 A.M. via Mansfield (about thirty miles out of the way). From there after a wait of four hours and fifty-eight minutes, a train left for New Washington, where it arrived at 4:27 P.M. If one did not care about returning the same day, there was a train in the morning at 8:33 A.M., which, with a transfer at Carrothers, brought one to New Washington fifty minutes later at 9:23 A.M. If there had been several daily connections like this one, we are sure that in our conversations with its older residents we might have found a soul who admitted to have gone from New Washington to Bucyrus by train. Horse and buggy and even walking were faster than the iron horse.

Since the railroads never served the needs of rural and small-town America, the people living in these areas rushed to the automobile as soon as it became a reliable means of transportation. This happened during the 1910s, when in the United States cars multiplied from 5 to 75 vehicles per 1,000 population. In 1910, when the automobile was still more of a recreational toy than a means of transportation, the states with the most automobiles on a per capita basis were the heavily urban ones such as the District of Columbia, California and Rhode Island. By 1920, when the car had become a means of transportation, the leading states were South Dakota, Iowa and Nebraska (with roughly as many motor vehicles per capita as the United Kingdom in 1960). Meantime, Rhode Island and the District of Columbia car-to-population ratio had fallen below the national average. Nine of the ten leading states were more rural than the national average. Today the sparsely settled states of the Mountain Region, Wyoming, Idaho, Montana and North Dakota, have, relatively speaking, the most cars, while urban areas such as New York State and the District of Columbia have the fewest.

During the 1920s, automobile ownership again more than doubled nationally. Now much of the growth was in urban areas, but least in the very large cities. Public transit also expanded its overall ridership, but not on a per capita basis. During the 1920s ridership grew at only about half the rate of the urban population.

During the economic stagnation of the 1930s, transit travel declined and auto travel remained about level. Then came the war and gasoline rationing. This brought a decline in auto travel and a new upsurge in transit travel to ridership levels which were on a per capita basis about equal to 1920. With the post-war years occurred not just the well-documented and much discussed decline in public transit, but also two technological transportation changes which have had major impact on urban America.

First, in nearly every city the last of the streetcars were replaced by buses. This trend began in the late twenties and continued through the thirties, but became a flood in the post-war period. Today 99 per cent of all transit mileage is by bus. There were clear economic advantages which made the conversion from streetcars to buses appealing to the transit companies. Track maintenance was eliminated, one mechanical failure did not halt the entire line, and buses were easily rerouted if demand shifted, or if a street became temporarily blocked due to a fire or other emergency. Then, too, the initial investment costs for buses were far lower than for tracked vehicles. Even though buses wore out sooner, and had higher seat – mile costs, these short-term investment savings were not inconsequential considerations to companies in poor financial health.

Even with these advantages, there is evidence that conscious attempts were made by automotive manufacturers and suppliers to speed the conversion from streetcars to buses. An anti-trust suit (United States versus National City Lines, Inc.) named General Motors, Firestone Tire, Standard Oil of California and Phillips Petroleum for being involved in just such an effort between the mid-thirties and mid-forties. The government argued that these manufacturers and suppliers tried to create an exclusive market for their products free from competition. It was alleged that these firms had bought a small midwestern transportation company, National City Lines, Inc., and used it as a holding company to obtain control of a sizable number of other transit companies in metropolitan areas throughout the Midwest and West. The individual transit companies then shifted their operations from streetcars to buses through loans from the same manufacturers and suppliers. These loans, it was alleged, required the transit companies to meet their present and future needs for rolling stock and supplies through purchases from the firms that extended the loans. It was the monopoly implications of these loans that caused the federal government to intercede and force the dissolution of the holding company. By that time, however, streetcars had been removed from a large number of metropolitan areas across the United States and replaced by buses.

Did transit passengers enjoy the switch to buses? Frankly, we doubt it. Letter after letter to local editors objected to the change. Buses were decried for their fumes, their jerky starts and stops, their lack of room and even their slow speed. Meanwhile, the transit companies marketed their buses by emphasizing the nice, new and shiny equipment, the safety of curbside stops, the 'modernness' and the speed. True, new buses usually compared favorably with old rickety streetcars, and the top speed of buses was greater than that of streetcars, but in heavy traffic this meant nothing. The streetcar operated in the center lane on a quasi private right-of-way and in heavy traffic this was an advantage over the bus in the curbside lane.

While transit riders may have grumbled, many in the general public championed the shift from streetcars to buses. The automobile riding public liked it. Buses inhibit smooth automobile flow less than streetcar tracks. Furthermore, in many places the removal of streetcar tracks permitted the widening of streets to accommodate the ever-growing auto traffic.

Shortly after the major conversion from streetcars to buses, the sharp decline in mass transit set in. While there were certainly other reasons for this decline, this juxtaposition still makes us wonder if the transit companies had not carried the principle of 'endurable hardship' a bit too far. When there is no competition, the operator's best economic strategy is to offer the cheapest service the public will endure, the 'endurable hardship'. To kick the public out of roomy but expensive streetcars into cramped, smelly, but cheap buses is a policy in full harmony with the 'endurable hardship' concept. But if the public has a choice, it might consider such transportation unendurable hardship, stay at home or travel by private automobile. Some members of the public had this choice and opted against riding the buses. From 1946 to the mid-sixties, the annual ridership of mass transit and the commuter trains in the U.S. dropped from over 23 billion to about 8.5 billion. All types of public transit were affected by this decline. However, the rapid transit systems, that is the subways, the elevated and the commuter trains, lost proportionately fewer riders than the motor buses, the streetcars and the trolley buses. These private right-of-way systems today account for about 20 per cent of all transit passengers compared to 12 per cent in 1946.

Many transit passengers felt they could kiss the slow, smelly bus goodby because of the other technological transportation changes that occurred in the post-war era. This change occurred in the automobile. Automatic transmission became commonplace, obsoleting the clutch pedal and persuading millions to become auto drivers. With an automatic transmission, driving in stop-and-go traffic is far more relaxing, and even the least experienced and most scared learner can start a car without making it buck like a Texas bronco. No longer was complex foot coordination required to drive a car, and many who previously had dreaded the thought of driving were now quite willing to take the plunge.

Just as the growth of tracked transportation enlarged and restructured the nineteenth-century city, so did the growth of rubber transportation, both public and private, enlarge and restructure the twentieth-century city. At least in the United States this enlarging and restructuring can be divided into two distinct periods, the period between the two world wars, and the period since the Second World War which is now coming to an end.

Street construction, particularly street surfacing, was the auto's first impact on the city's structure. Until the advent of motorized transportation, road and street construction had been adapted to the needs of horse transportation. This meant that, for maximum traction without slipping, the surface had to give the horse a way to anchor its hoof, without unduly increasing the friction between the heavily laden wagon wheel and the road. Dirt roads met the horses' requirement for traction, but not the wagon's requirement for minimum friction, particularly not in wet weather when dirt roads turned to mud lanes. However, since these were the cheapest roads and at least met minimum needs, they were also the most prevalent. Even better were broken stone, gravel or any other low-type surfaced road. If traffic was relatively light and the loads not too heavy, these surfaces would not rut under the pressure of wagon wheels and the surface was still rough enough to prevent the horses from slipping. But with heavy traffic, these light-surfaced roads soon rutted. Hard-surfaced roads were needed that could resist heavy traffic and inclement weather and still prevent horses from slipping. Cobblestone met these specifications best. The stones guaranteed low friction between wheel and road, and the cracks provided anchorage for hoofs. Unfortunately, no one really liked these roads, except the teamsters who hauled the very heavy loads. To pave a road with cobblestone was expensive and the end product terribly noisy. The beat of iron hoofs against hard smooth stones generates an awful racket.

Motor-vehicle transportation with rubber tires functions best on high-grade, hard-surfaced, smoothly paved roads, and worst on wet dirt roads, where the wheels tend to slip rather than provide forward motion to the vehicle. For all practical purposes, wet dirt roads were impassible for autos, while horses still could traverse them even if they could pull only reduced loads. The hard-surfaced smooth roads which the motorists and truckers wanted were not cobblestone roads, but the much cheaper asphalt and cement roads.

In the nineteenth century, roads in the United States as a class, both urban and rural, were far inferior to European roads. This at least is the opinion of Dean Shaler of Harvard University, who also believed that by the 1890s there was a strong movement afoot to remedy this situation. As the Dean, writing in 1896, puts it so charmingly:

The historian of this country for the century which is now drawing to a close is likely to note the fact that the people of the United States bore in a singularly patient manner with the evils arising from poor carriage roads until near the end of the tenth decade, and that they then were suddenly aroused to a sense of the sore tax the ill condition of these necessary features of civilization had long inflicted upon them.[2]

It is hard to pinpoint the source of this early pressure, which ante-dated the automobile by a number of years, but it is certain that there was wide support for better roads. Since these roads did not compete with the railroads but supplied access to them, there was no objection to better roads by the influential rail lobby. In the urban areas the pressure for better roads came not just from the bicyclists but also from the merchants in the outlying residential neighborhoods and their suppliers. Another source of the 'arousal' were the small towns and rural communities who were so badly served by the railroads. All these pressures led the U.S. government in 1894 to create an Office of Road Inquiry. This office initiated experiments and conducted inquiries about the best methods of road building.

While the motoring public and their clubs did not start the pressure for better roads, there is no doubt that they added fuel and kept up the

2. N. S. Shaler, *American Highways*, The Century Co., New York, 1896, page 1

pressure until not only all highways but also every city street and farm road had been drained, graveled and paved.

The pressure for better roads by the motoring public and their allies did not stop with the improvement and paving of existing road mileage. Starting in the 1920s, pressure was exerted on the larger cities to build exclusive automobile roads, parkways. These roads, which were the first limited-access roads, were neither planned nor designed to handle the morning and evening rush-hour traffic, nor to facilitate the suburbanite's city access. On the contrary, they were built strictly for the recreation of the city dwellers. With these roads, the motoring urban public could take pleasant spins through the city's open spaces and parks, and on out into the countryside. Naturally, these roads were directed toward the nearest open country, that is, the areas between the points of the tracked city's star pattern. To enhance the motorist's joy in using these recreational facilities, bus and truck traffic was barred from the new parkways.

In addition to these new roads, the 1930s, under the impetus of federal public works programs, also saw the rebuilding of many city streets and intersections to accommodate the ever-growing automobile traffic.

As far as land use changes are concerned, the first effects of the automobile did not develop in the cities themselves, but in the railroad suburbs that surrounded them. When these suburbs were laid out and developed, the ads proclaimed that every new subdivision was within easy walking distance of the railroad station, even if this distance turned out to be a mile or more. In the 1920s, these pretenses were dropped. The old railroad suburbs expanded well beyond easy walking distance to the depot and the lots became larger. Whereas in 1900 no one dared to advertise a home that was not in easy walking distance, by the 1920s no one dared to offer a new home that did not have off-street parking, and it nearly always featured a garage. While cars were widely used to get to the depot, there was only limited auto commuting to the cities. As these suburbs grew, their shopping facilities grew also, but only at a rate compensatory with the population growth, and only as an enlargement of the already existing business districts.

The big changes in metropolitan land use came in the post-Second World War period. These years brought with them an enormous demand for the metropolitan areas to grow in size. The impetus for this growth came partially from the natural growth in population and the virtual housing moratorium of the depression and war years. Far more important, however, was the accelerated migration of machine-replaced farm laborers to the cities, and the desire of the older city population to escape in ever-larger numbers from the dirt and the crowding of the cities to the open spaces of the suburbs. These pressures were helped by the U.S. government's policy to aid farmers in mechanizing their operations, and the policy of helping potential home buyers through guaranteed home mortgages which required only 10 to 20 per cent down payments, and in the case of veterans frequently no down payment at all. The cities and the old railroad and streetcar suburbs could not accommodate all this growth. New open spaces were needed. Since any family that could afford a house was also expected to own a car, any open space would do that had a road connection to the city. If it was close to the city, so much the better. Under this influence the areas between the points of the tracked city's star pattern became available for settlement. The once recreational parkways became commuter roads, while the star-shaped tracked city transformed itself into the sprawling rubber city whose boundaries are undefinable.

With the car, where every place is accessible as long as it is served by a road, the layout of highways and other transportation facilities becomes far less a determiner of land use than other factors. A careful look at suburbia proves this point. While in the popular mind there may exist a stereotype of what suburbia is like, the most amazing factor is not how much one suburb is just like the next, because everywhere people watch the same television shows and use the same deodorants, but how vastly these suburbs differ from one another even if they are located right next to each other. In the urban areas of the United States, the differences from municipality to municipality are greater today than they have ever been, and they are greater than in any other nation since the beginning of mankind. The suburban towns today are not only differentiated by income and race, but by many other factors as well. There are suburbs for the young and the elderly; there are suburbs for the college-educated and those who didn't graduate from high school; there are suburbs for one-family homes and apartment houses, for the professional and the unskilled. There are suburbs that have good shopping and those that have none, suburbs where industry flourishes and where there is none. Finally, there are suburbs that represent each and every shade of wealth from stark poverty to utmost luxury. At no times in the history of man was such a variety possible.

In older days even suburbs with mansions had their poor, for the rich required servants that lived in. As a result, the rich lived in close proximity to at least some of the poor. Today, live-in servants are a rarity, and the few houseworkers who still ply the trade are more likely than not commuters. In former days, even the richest of suburbs had many modest homes for the artisans, the store clerks, the firemen, the policemen, the schoolteachers and all others who furnished the support a community of large mansions required. Today, a suburban town can consist of nothing but mansions and get away with it. All the town has to do is zone its entire residential land into two-acre lots, ban industry and commerce, and establish sufficiently tough building ordinances to assure that nothing but expensive homes are built. If the neighboring suburbs have stores and gas stations, one can go there for shopping, and the civil servants the community requires can jolly well commute from one of these surrounding towns. Since all classes are willing to commute, purely residential towns of modest homes are possible too, and many exist. In many states, municipalities can survive financially with no or only little industry and commerce. If their per capita real-estate tax base drops too low, the states, through 'equalizing' tax-aid programs, will supply the missing revenue to the municipalities. The automobile, modern home appliances and government policies all have conspired to make a reality of evermore specialized suburban municipalities, which rightly can say that their problems are not those of their neighbors while blandly forgetting that they cannot survive without these neighbors.

If one looks at these modern suburbs through the cold facts of scientific data, the differences are statistically significant, amazing and alarming. Oliver P. Williams and some of his colleagues at the Fels Institute made a statistical study of the municipalities in the four eastern Pennsylvania counties that surround Philadelphia[3]. In this

3. Oliver P. Williams, Harold Herman, Charles S. Liebman, Thomas R. Dye, *Suburban Differences and Metropolitan Policies, A Philadelphia Story*, University of Pennsylvania Press, Philadelphia, 1965. All data are for 1959 or 1960.

study the research team distinguished between the 'suburban' area, the communities forming a contiguous built-up area around Philadelphia, and the 'semi-urban' area that lay beyond. This latter area included rural townships as well as built-up towns, of which some were old farm villages and others were mainly industrial communities. As part of their study, the research team showed that there were greater statistical variations among the 'suburban' communities than the 'semi-urban' communities with respect to age, education, occupation, wealth, property value and real-estate devoted to residential' use. Thus, the suburban towns varied more among each other than a group of municipalities that consisted of rural farm land and small commercial and industrial cities.

Philadelphia's suburbs present a sort of 'social cafeteria', but – with one important proviso – for whites only. Economics aside, whites can 'choose' the type of community they want and the range of choices is wide. Do they want a youthful community? In one suburb, 40 per cent of all adults are between 25 and 35. If they prefer a more mature environment, another town has only 9 per cent of its adults in the young married bracket. A well-educated environment? Philadelphia has a suburb where over 70 per cent of all adults had attended college. If education is not the style, another suburb has no more than 1 in 40 who had been to college. Do they want to live among professionals, managers and salesmen? In one community, 5 of every 6 employed men have such occupations, but in another it was only 1 in 16.

How expensive should the homes be in the 'chosen' town? Values ranged from an average of $5,600 in one town to over $24,000 in another. Do they care about a town's tax base? Here too wide choices are possible. In one town the base was $1,700 per person, while in another it was over $12,000. Do they prefer an industrial and commercial town or a residential community? One suburb's taxable real-estate was 87 per cent industrial and commercial. Another's was 100 per cent residential. Although in this suburb one could apparently buy neither a loaf of bread nor a gallon of gas, the community was a legal political entity.

Unfortunately the study does not discuss ethnic differences, which may be less pronounced today than in the streetcar days. Race, however, is another matter. In Philadelphia, a fourth of the population was black, but in the suburbs only a twentieth. Even this small percentage was by no means evenly distributed; one suburb was three-fourths black, but in nearly half the suburbs blacks formed less than one per cent of the population. All these data are from 1960. Blacks made no progress in penetrating suburbia during the 1950s, in fact they lost ground, and the story was not much different in the 1960s.

The Philadelphia story is neither unique nor a tale peculiar to the East Coast of the United States. In the West are also cities of vast age differences, and we presume of vast social differences as well. According to the 1970 U.S. Census, the median age in the Los Angeles area was 28 years, but within the area wide variations existed. There were youthful towns, towns for the more mature, and towns devoted to the aged. There were Simi Valley, Compton, West Puenta Valley and Valinda, where half the population was below 21, and South San Jose Hills, where at 17 one belonged to the older half of the population. Meanwhile there were also such mature towns as Arcadia, Alhambra, Burbank, Glendale and Santa Monica, where the median age ranged between 35 and 40, or Beverly Hills and Palm Springs, where half the population was over 45. Finally, there were towns where most were senior citizens. In Hemmet the median age was 63.9 and in LaGuna Hills, a community of some 13,000, one belonged still to the younger half at 68.

The smorgasbord character of the U.S. metropolitan suburbs applies increasingly to the city as well. Today's inner city population is neither a microcosm nor a random sample of the metropolitan population. With the influx of former farm labor – which is predominantly black or Spanish-speaking – and the outflow of the white middle class, the inner city population reflects the overall metropolitan area neither in racial and ethnic background nor income. More of the inner city's population belongs to minority groups, is old and young adult, and is mostly poorer than in the rest of the metropolitan area.

As more people moved to suburbia and commuted to the city by car, rush-hour congestion steadily increased, and shouts for better road transportation to the inner city became the cry of the day. These pressures led in the 1950s and 60s to the building of six-, eight- and ten-lane freeways. Suburbanites wanted these roads to get into the city, and business in the city wanted the roads to 'preserve' downtown. Since the Second World War, business in suburbia has grown at a much faster rate than in the inner city, and in some inner cities business has in fact declined. Many factors contributed to this growth pattern. Suburban land was cheaper, far out-weighing the extra trucking costs that such a location may entail. Since more and more workers commuted by car and lived in suburbia, there was a growing labor force locally available. Where business involved retailing, a suburban location might even be closer to the customers than a city location. While one suburban department store can never serve the entire metropolitan area – as a downtown department store used to do – with the general growth of the metropolitan population, several somewhat smaller suburban retail branches might profitably replace the one large downtown store.

The urban freeways were supposed to steady the economy of the inner city, and preserve the spatial arrangements of the tracked city with business at the center, surrounded by an industrial belt and residents of progressively greater wealth in spikes beyond the belt. In reality, where freeways were built and became the dominant transportation arteries, they completely destroyed this pattern. With urban freeways, any trip during off hours was quicker and more convenient than during rush hours. This is directly contrary to the prevailing pattern in the tracked city, where rush-hour travel due to more frequent schedules involved less waiting and delays than off-hour travel. What was the result of this reversal? Instead of remaining 'downtown', industry and business found with the freeways even less reason to locate in the central part of the city than they had in the earlier days when car transportation became plentiful. Unless many employees needed daily face-to-face contact with other firms or clients that were downtown, it was just as easy – and probably more economical – to locate at the outskirts, near the boss's home, and come to town only during the day to meet colleague Joe or client Moneybags for lunch. The flight of corporate headquarters from Manhattan to suburbia (see Table 1) would never have occurred if there were not easier access through the Interstate Highway System to Manhattan during the day than during rush-hours. Of the thirty-three large corporations that left or were about to leave Manhattan between 1967 and 1971, only six left the New York metropolitan region. All the others went to suburbs with limited-access highway connections to New York. Naturally, not all the

Table 1: Manhattan's dropouts

Between 1967 and 1970 these companies moved their headquarters out of Manhattan:

Company	1970 sales (in millions)	New location
American Can	$1,838	Greenwich, Conn.
Avco	758	Greenwich
Bangor Punta	342	Greenwich
BASF (U.S. Division)	56	Parsippany, N.J.
Columbia Gas System	823	Wilmington, Del.
CPC (Corn Products)	1,376	Englewood Cliffs, N.J.
Flintkote	355	White Plains, N.Y.
Foster Wheeler	391	Livingston, N.J.
Hooker Chemical	N.A.*	Stamford, Conn.
Howmet	250	Greenwich
ICI America	67	Stamford
M.W. Kellogg	N.A.*	Houston, Texas
Lone Star Cement	265	Greenwich
Lummus	192	Bloomfield, N.J.
Metro-Goldwyn-Mayer	171	Culver City, Calif.
Microdot	155	Greenwich
Olin	1,125	Stamford
Panhandle Eastern Pipe Line	419	Houston
PepsiCo	N.A.*	Purchase, N.Y.
States Marine International	123	Stamford
Union Camp	462	Wayne, N.J.
U.S. Tobacco	86	Greenwich

In 1971 the following major corporations were in the process of moving their headquarters out of Manhattan:

Company	1970 sales (in millions)	Destination
AMF	$636	White Plains
Chesebrough-Pond's	261	Greenwich
Combustion Engineering	957	Stamford
Continental Oil	2,964	Stamford
Gen. Tel. & El.	3,439	Stamford
Great Northern Paper	355	Stamford

Table 1 (contd)

Company	1970 sales (in millions)	Destination
Ingersoll-Rand	766	Woodcliff Lake, N.J.
Kraftco	737	Chicago
Richardson-Merrell	381	Southern Connecticut
Shell Oil	4,299	Houston
Stauffer Chemical	483	Westport, Conn.

* Figure not available.
Source: *Time* Magazine, 26 April 1971, p. 87.

employees of a company live in the same sector of the metropolitan area. Thus when a company leaves downtown and moves to suburbia, the commute distance becomes shorter for the president and those who had the good sense to live in the same sector as he did, while the commute distances of those living in the inner city or other sections of the metropolitan area become longer. The lengthening nearly always outbalances the shortening. Worse yet, daytime travel, measured in trip mileage and trip times, will increase sharply. The freeways thus act as positive traffic generators without 'preserving' anything.

With motor vehicles and freeways, transportation has become so plentiful and so universal that the transportation arteries no longer give a structuring to the urban environment. Anything within ten or twenty miles is as available, as easy to reach, as anything next door. With transportation furnishing no structure but only a vague size limitation, cities have grown enormously, and today it is frequently fifty to a hundred miles from one end of the built-up area to the other. Only in the rarest of cases are these metropolitan areas one political unit, and in the case of the largest cities such as New York, Tokyo, Paris or London, never. The question of where the metropolitan area ends has become a very real one. It is unclear how far out one has to go to encompass the population that functions as part of the metropolis without claiming metropolitan orientation for those who have no daily contact with the metropolis. Obviously there are no sharp limits. Any political or planning boundary will be arbitrary. What is even more significant, with the decline of the central business district, many metropolitan areas are in fact centerless. This is not limited to Los Angeles and the

Rhine–Ruhr district. There still may be an area where there is greater employment density than anywhere else in the metropolis, but ever fewer of the residents have any contact with this area. Their economic, social and political lives gravitate around some 'section' of the glob we call a metropolitan area, and have little or nothing to do with other 'sections' of the metropolitan area. In the New York area, many Long Island and North Jersey residents hardly ever get to Manhattan. Their relation to the center of the metropolitan area is thus tenuous at best. But worse yet, the Long Island residents who have never been to North Jersey, and vice versa, are counted in the tens if not hundreds of thousands. What orientation in common have these people socially, economically or politically to classify them as residents of the New York metropolitan area, and through this distinguish them from the non-metropolitan population, or the residents of the Philadelphia, Boston, Chicago or Los Angeles areas?

The metropolitan areas of today reflect the same problems that plagued our major cities a hundred years ago. Local transportation then as now was not good enough to accommodate the pressure for urban growth. At that time living conditions in the cities steadily deteriorated and New York, Boston and Philadelphia each lost its integrated urban unity as satellite cities arose in the environs. The same occurs today. The continuing pressure for growth in the major urban areas is faster than present transportation can support. Even with freeways we are unable to travel in one hour from one end of these built-up areas to the other. As a result, what once was economically and socially a somewhat unified area begins to break apart.

Changes during the past ten years in the U.S. Bureau of Census' Standard Metropolitan Statistical Areas (SMSAs) portray this phenomenon. The SMSAs are defined roughly as one or more central cities of at least 50,000 and their counties, together with the surrounding counties in which over 15 per cent of the workers commute to the counties which contain the central cities. The SMSAs were originally defined in 1949. Since then, as new census data became available, the New York SMSA was broken up into five distinct SMSAs: New York, Nassau-Suffolk, Jersey City, Newark and Patterson-Clifton-Passaic. The Chicago SMSA was split into Chicago and Gary-Hammond-East Chicago. The Los Angeles SMSA lost Orange County which formed the new Anaheim-Santa Ana-Garden Grove SMSA. The San Francisco SMSA lost Solano County which with Napa County formed the Valleyo-Napa SMSA. Even the much smaller Wheeling SMSA was split to form the Wheeling SMSA and the Steubenville-Weirton SMSA.

By cold statistical measures, these split-offs are perfectly good metropolitan areas. Yet we wonder if they have the cohesiveness and the richness of life once associated with a metropolitan city! Even though these split-offs are large – four have over a million population – we wonder if they are not really 'sub'-metropolitan areas to the older centers. The Census Bureau is wondering too and is groping for better definitions. But if these areas are only 'sub'-metropolitan areas, and not true metropolitan areas, their behavior patterns show that they have lost the ease of access to the old centers which they once had – and even to the nation as a whole. With the exception of Newark, these areas have no scheduled airline service.

Though the larger metropolitan areas appear to be breaking up, the automobile does not only disperse man's activities; it also concentrates them. In the United States, where there were once many institutions, today with automobile transportation there are fewer and larger institutions. The best example is provided by the schools. For every elementary and high school pupil of 1930, there are two pupils today, but for every two schools today, there were five schools in 1930. These fewer but larger schools can offer a wider curriculum and can use expensive instructional aids and materials more efficiently. Thus, the one- and two-room schoolhouses were closed and replaced by consolidated schools. With school buses it is no longer necessary that schools are within walking distance of the child's home.

Larger hospitals, again within reason, are more efficient than smaller ones and can offer better services. Since 1930, the U.S. population increased by just 60 per cent, while hospital admissions increased over 300 per cent. Then only one baby in three was born in a hospital; today all but one in forty is. Still, since 1930 the number of hospitals has grown by a paltry 6 per cent. Many new municipalities have no hospital facilities at all. Without the ready availability of automobile transportation, this concentration of hospital services would not have been possible.

Since 1930, there has also been a marked reduction in food stores. Where once there were three stores, there are two today. Yesterday most food was bought at neighborhood groceries and most housewives shopped daily for otherwise the load was too great to carry. Today, many households shop only once a week. The refrigerator permits the preserving of food at home and the automobile gives the capability to carry large quantities. The self-service supermarkets with low mark-ups became possible when people were able to shop for large quantities of food at a time. It is no accident that food prices are highest where customers walk to the store and buy in small quantities.

Concentration in business and service and dispersal in living are the hallmarks of the modern metropolis. Unfortunately, the automobile is much more efficient at dispersal than at concentration. The former requires only roads, the latter, roads and parking places. It is this need for parking facilities that more than anything else led to the dispersal of businesses and industries all through the metropolitan area. Since the size of individual plants or enterprises has not shrunk but grown, the number of enterprises that can collocate without traffic jams is becoming smaller and smaller. As the free-enterprise, industrial city broke up the tailor's row and dyer's corner of the medieval city, the automobile today is breaking up the central business district of our streetcar cities into small business and industrial sections throughout the metropolitan area.

Still, even within these sections a reconcentration is beginning to take shape. During the past decade ever larger shopping centers and industrial parks have appeared. Industries, like residents, will not locate just anywhere in the metropolitan area, but will try to choose sites that have access to the same services and labor force as their competitors. While in the 1950s electronic companies around Boston, New York, Philadelphia and San Francisco spread their plants nearly randomly over fairly large suburban areas, by the mid 1960s new plants and offices tended to locate as close as possible to established facilities. This was particularly true of the newer and smaller companies. These companies in fact are willing to pay rent premiums to be as close to their competitors as possible. The reason is simple. Any small new development or manufacturing company must farm out, often on short notice and under severe time pressures, a lot of its service requirements from typing, to duplicating, to drafting, to part machining. Similarly these companies need to purchase office supplies, components and tools. The smaller the company, the less capital it has, the more frequently it must make purchases. Thus to minimize transportation requirements during the business day, a physical concentration of the smaller suburban industrial and service establishments is occurring.

The rubber city, characterized by the dispersal of all activity centers, is approaching its limits, and a metropolitan area with new forms of concentration is beginning to emerge. Exactly what the future urban patterns will be is uncertain. One fact is clear: like all other urban patterns the new pattern will be shaped by the availability of transportation and the priorities assigned to different trip purposes. The diminishing interest in urban freeways and the growing interest in rapid transit systems with stations every three to five miles and more, as in the new San Francisco Bay area system, may well hold the key to the structure of the metropolitan area of the future.

CHAPTER 5

The Market City Prior to the Automobile

A secret dread of urban commuters is the thought that some fine day there will be such a terrific traffic jam that they won't be able to go home. In Boston, a metropolitan area of 2.5 million, this horror came to pass for many on 30 December 1963. It was a Monday, the sun shone all day, the streets were clear and dry, and the temperature never climbed above freezing. Who would have expected trouble that fine day? Christmas had been the week before and many people were still on vacation. During the previous week there had also been a snow–storm and generally miserable weather which kept most people close to home. By Monday, the pent-up population exploded. The commuters went to work, and all others decided to get out of the house as well. On such a fine day, why not go shopping, take advantage of the post-Christmas sales, spend the Christmas money, exchange Aunt Martha's gift for something more suitable, or just look at the Christmas decorations? Unfortunately too many headed for downtown Boston. The merchants cheerfully reported the best post-Christmas shopping day ever, and the exhausted police gloomily the worst traffic jam ever. Over 100 thousand cars headed for an area that had only 37 thousand 'legal' parking places. By two in the afternoon, the city was clogged with double- and triple-parked cars. Nothing moved. By nine in the evening, the traffic was still snarled. During that short but seemingly interminable period of time, the absurdity of modern urban transportation was driven into the consciousness of every participant. There they were, these moderns, with their public street transit systems and most importantly their private automobiles. They had more mobility than any previous generation could imagine, yet they could not move. They could not even eat or take other creature comforts. How could such an impressive array of tools for mobility achieve zero access? The answer is at once both simple and complex.

In a simple sense, the capacity of the existing transportation system was overtaxed and could not supply the access the citizens of the Boston metropolitan area were seeking. But the answer is also complex. More transportation capacity – more mobility – might in fact have led to an even worse traffic jam and provided even less access to the central core of the metropolitan area. Transportation and urban growth go hand-in-hand. Where transportation and land use are primarily dictated by the market place, that is occur in response to the demands of consumers or buyers, a city in the age of private automobile transportation must sooner or later drown in its excessive mobility. Boston, in this respect, is no different from any other city.

Throughout its history, at least until the late 1960s, Boston responded to the pressures of the market. These pressures reflected not the long-run concerns necessary for the smooth growth and functioning of a large, high-density population concentration, but the immediate short-run needs of the actors at a point in time. While economists would say that a 'properly functioning' market would evaluate both long- and short-term effects, they would also concede that few markets function 'properly'. It is this 'improperly functioning' marketplace that shaped the Boston metropolitan area, and consequently it is there that we must look to see how mobility could take precedence over access.

What is today the heart of downtown Boston is considered by most to be the original point of settlement, but it is not. Rather, the first site chosen by that band of Puritans who founded the Massachusetts Bay Colony in 1630 was across the harbor at the foot of Bunker Hill, in what is today Charlestown. This was clearly a superior choice. The site sits at the junction of two rivers on a good harbor opening to the sea. It also had much space and good overland connections to the interior. Had the settlers remained here and begun building a city from this spot, the history of Boston would have been far different, geographically and perhaps economically and politically. But they did not remain. The shallow springs of the Charlestown area had brackish water, and, rather than dig deeper wells, these first settlers relocated across the harbor on the Shawmut Peninsula, where there was an adequate fresh-water spring. The Shawmut Peninsula is the piece of real-estate on which modern downtown Boston sits.

The peninsula was an unlikely location for the focal point of a major metropolitan region. In the seventeenth century, the peninsula was about a mile and a half long and a mile across at its widest point. It was connected to the mainland by a narrow isthmus, the 'neck', a thin marshy strip of land less than 500 feet wide. While the acreage of the peninsula was sufficient for a fair-sized city, much of the land was unusable. The shorelines were marshy and the center was dominated

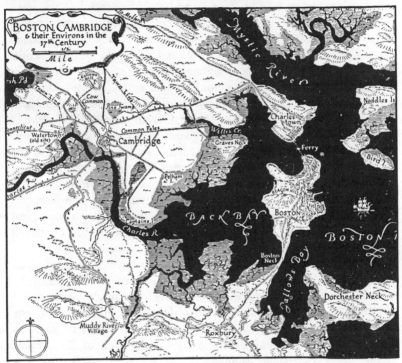

Map 1

by three craggy hills, the Trimountains: Mount Vernon, Beacon Hill and Pemberton Hill.

The shift to the Shawmut forced a shift in economic emphasis. Had the Boston Puritans remained in the Charlestown area, the settlers could have looked inward as well as out to the sea. They could have exploited the land in farming and timber harvesting; they could have become shipbuilders and manufacturers; they could have become fishermen. They could have engaged in all these activities, as did the

Puritan colonists who settled Salem, Quincy and the other coastal towns. Settlement on the Shawmut Peninsula foreclosed these options, and Boston in the seventeenth and eighteenth century could grow only as a seaport and trading center.

Maybe because they had no other choices, the Boston settlers became excellent merchants and sea traders and quickly developed the town into the foremost shipping and trading center along the eastern seaboard. In fact, Boston's traders were so good that their trade soon expanded beyond the East Coast, to the Caribbeans, to Africa and to Europe. These successes brought the fledgling traders of the New World into face-to-face competition with the old-established merchants of London and Liverpool. As so often happens where there is economic competition from an upstart, the rules of the game were 'adjusted'. In the mid eighteenth century, the British merchants prevailed upon Parliament to change the trading and taxing regulations to the detriment of the colonial merchants. The squeezed colonials took revenge by becoming early and fierce supporters of the thirteen colonies' bid for independence. One wonders if the Bostonians would have been quite such ferocious advocates of independence, rebellion and revolution had the original settlers remained in Charlestown and developed a broader-based economy.

Boston was land-poor until the end of the nineteenth century. Well over half of today's central business district is built on filled land. The lack of land put a noticeable constraint on Boston's growth from around 1800 on. After the revolution, the growth in economic activity in the city jumped considerably with the removal of the British restraint on trade. Before the revolution in 1765, the population of Boston was 15,520. After Independence in 1790, the population was 18,320, a modest growth. However, by 1800, it had risen to 24,937. In annual terms, the growth rate in the 25-year period from 1765 to 1790 was .6 per cent per year. However, between 1790 and 1800, it jumped to just over 3 per cent per year and continued at this rate until 1830. The expanding post-war economy brought an influx of people into the city and created new fortunes in shipping and trading. Thus, pressures were great to expand business and public properties as well as residential areas. The flat and dry regions of the Shawmut Peninsula could not accommodate this growth and the settlement began to spread into the rougher topographical areas of the Trimountains, particularly Beacon Hill.

The first thrust in this direction came in 1795, when the new State House, the administrative center of the Commonwealth of Massachusetts, was built in John Hancock's cow pasture on Beacon Hill. The State House needed no ready harbor access and could easily occupy the town's most remote location. Mount Vernon, next to the State House, was purchased by a syndicate of real-estate speculators under Harrison Gray Otis. This syndicate removed between fifty and sixty feet from the top of Mount Vernon and used the earth to fill some of their other properties in the marshes along Charles Street. This land on Mount Vernon and Charles Street was sold to the prospering merchants of newly independent Boston for house lots. In the next several decades, more of the Trimountains was removed and used for land fill.

The tools available to create useful land – pick, shovel, and horse-drawn wagon – were cumbersome. Thus Boston also tried to gain access to additional land beyond the Shawmut Peninsula. To the north, bridges were built across the Charles River in 1786, 1793 and 1809. These provided access to East Cambridge and the mainland beyond it. The town fathers decided in 1801 to develop the public land to the south that lay beyond the neck and bordered on the town of Roxbury. Meanwhile, the Otis Syndicate tried to extend Boston to the southeast, where across the mud flats of Gallows or South Bay was the Dorchester Neck. The syndicate bought this land and in 1804 had it annexed to Boston by the State Legislature. Once this was accomplished the syndicate constructed a toll bridge across the flats to the area which is now called South Boston.

The Charles River bridges helped to settle East Cambridge with the typical characteristics of a faubourg, but the two real-estate undertakings to the south and southeast were premature. As they had no good overland transportation any distance too onerous to walk had to be avoided. While South Boston was really not too far from the city center, the toll bridge foreclosed it to those who might have exchanged a long walk for cheap land. The distance across the Neck to the public land on the Roxbury line was just too far in the early 1800s to be attractive to anyone. The scarcity of transportation in Federal Boston made growth through land fill the economically most feasible option.

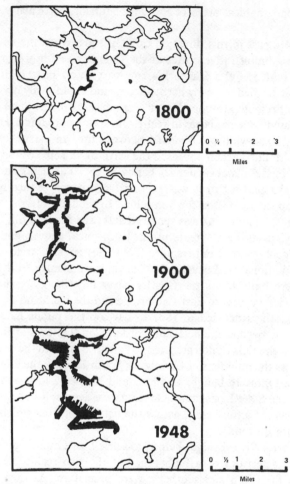

Map 2. *The growth of Boston's shoreline and port areas (source: Greater Boston Development Committee Inc.*, Surging Cities, *1948)*

Beginning in 1812 and culminating about 1824, Beacon Hill was cut down by about a third of its height. The land from the hill was used to fill in the Mill Pond at the bottom of the hill, the site where today the Massachusetts General Hospital and the city's jail are located.

In the two decades from 1810 until 1830, the population of Boston increased by 82 per cent to 61,392. This created pressures to use land at a further distance from the city center. In 1828 a second bridge to South Boston was constructed. This bridge, unlike the first, was toll-free and built by the city. Pressure for space had grown sufficiently to justify politically the expenditure of public funds to gain access to a piece of nearby vacant land. With the free bridge South Boston became another locational choice for all the new business enterprises, their owners and employees, which did not need to be near the port. The early real-estate speculators had been correct in anticipating the direction of the expansion, but they erred in terms of the market the area could attract. When the land on the Roxbury end of the Neck finally developed in the 1820s and 1830s, it attracted the same type of land use and population as South Boston.

Meanwhile, in these years of expansion, Boston's most successful citizens were also searching for new sites for their mansions. One of these searchers was the China trade merchant and former soldier Thomas Handasyd Perkins. As his biographers tell it:

For over thirty years, Colonel Perkins lived on one side or the other of Pearl Street. It was a highly convenient situation Just a few blocks walk to the east brought him to his counting room. The same distance north and he was on State Street, where he could share in the gossip and schemes of the merchants on 'Change. Beautiful shade trees and lovely gardens gave the street a delightful rural aspect. At the end of the street, across High Street, was the shore. A short after-dinner stroll would bring the Colonel up on Fort Hill from whose height he could scan the harbor for late arriving ships and enjoy the scenic view of Boston Bay. . . .

But time was bringing changes to this pleasant area. Commercial Boston was spreading out in every direction from State Street. Gradually Pearl Street was being engulfed. Houses were even being built on Fort Hill. Boston's expanding overseas trade, to which the Colonel himself contributed in no small measure, required warehouses and these were pushing in from the waterfront. . . .

As the slums moved toward Pearl Street, as the commercial growth encroached upon it, the Colonel began to get restless and started looking for a better place to live.[1]

1. Carl Seaburg and Stanley Paterson, *Merchant Prince of Boston: Colonel T. H. Perkins, 1764–1854*, Harvard University Press, Cambridge, 1971, pages 375–6.

In 1831, the Colonel found what he sought. He built his new home on Temple Place. This site was a mere 1,400 feet inland from his Pearl Street residence. In walking Boston, a move of a quarter mile was sufficient to escape from a declining 'neighborhood' to the city's best residential 'area'.

Although the population growth was high in the four decades between 1790 and 1830, it did not match the growth of the next two decades from 1830 to 1850. In that period the population more than doubled, growing at an annual rate of 4 per cent, from 61,392 to 136,881 souls. This growth was both facilitated and caused by the changes in transportation and land patterns.

Overland transportation was expensive, but overwater transport was never quite that dear. Thus where possible the latter was used in the movement of goods and people, especially after the advent of steam ferry boats. In the Boston area this led to the development of East Boston in the years after 1830. East Boston is located across Boston Harbor to the east of Charlestown. Back in 1830, East Boston was still an island – Noddle's Island – disconnected from the mainland to the north by tidal flats. The Sumner family owned nearly the entire island. To exploit the island's potential value as a real-estate development, the family incorporated the East Boston Company in 1833 and laid out the land in lots, streets, squares, wharves and commercial areas. The following year the East Boston Company began regular ferry service between East Boston and Boston's North End, the northern tip of the Shawmut Peninsula. The opening of the ferry service was timed to coincide with the start of passenger and freight service by the Eastern Railroad. This company had a charter to furnish rail service between Boston and the coastal towns to the northeast. To enter Boston from the northeast required the crossing of several rivers and mudflats, an expensive undertaking for the fledgling railroad. The company, therefore, decided to build a causeway between the mainland to the north and Noddle's Island, and make East Boston its southern terminal. With ferry service to Boston and rail service to the North Shore communities, East Boston and its port facilities prospered. By 1857, its population was 16,600, almost a tenth of the total Boston population. The assessed taxable valuation of the area had grown from $60,000 in 1833 to $806,000 in 1835 and to $8,000,000 in 1856.

In spite of the success of the East Boston real-estate development venture, the ferry proved to be a financial failure. The service had been started by the East Boston Company with two steam boats, the *East Boston* and the *Maverick*. In 1835, the company sold the ferry franchise to a new company composed of some of its own stockholders for $66,000. The facilities had originally cost the East Boston Company $141,861. In its first year under the new operators the ferry lost $22,000. The Eastern Railroad, unable to obtain permission to operate its own ferry, bought a majority of the ferry stock, paying $51,000 for just over half of it. By 1838, the ferry was once again losing money and the railroad and the East Boston Company each had to put up $5,000 to cover the losses incurred. In the period 1839–40, the East Boston Company took over the administration of the ferry. During the ten-year period 1842–52, the management was split between the East Boston Company and the Eastern Railroad. In that time, the ferry lost $29,000. An attempt to revitalize the operation was made in 1852, when a new company purchased the ferry and franchise from the old company for $200,000. It purchased new boats, ran one all night and three during the day. In addition, it obtained a new, more centrally located, landing place in Boston. In 1853 it was able to show a profit of $20,000. At about the same time a group of East Boston residents began running their own ferry. The competition proved too much for the fragile business and as a result both companies lost money. To cover their losses the two companies petitioned the city to pay the maintenance expenses of the ferry docks. These costs amounted to about $6,000 per company per year. The city delayed action on these requests and the lines raised their tolls in 1856. By this time the East Boston Company had developed all its real-estate and was no longer interested in low ferry tolls to induce would-be buyers. The Eastern Railroad had also lost interest in the ferries. Two years before the railroad had built a line directly into Boston. Ultimately, the city purchased the ferries and began absorbing the deficit in the municipal budget.

The impact of the ferries on the extension of Boston was minor compared to that of the railroads. In Boston, as elsewhere, the era of the early railroads occurred simultaneously with a surge in industrialization and the migration of large population groups to the cities. Since these trends interact it is difficult to tell which comes first – the railroads, the industrialization or the population influx. The railroads, though they may not have started the growth cycle in Boston, were a necessary spark for accelerated growth.

The first steam railroad incorporated in the Boston area was the Boston & Lowell Railroad in 1830. In 1831, the Boston & Worcester and the Boston & Providence followed suit. All three lines started service during the summer of 1835. All three built their terminals at the edge of the then built-up area. And all three entered the Shawmut Peninsula across the water, the Boston & Lowell from the north on a bridge that crossed the Charles River, the Providence line from the southwest through Roxbury and on a causeway across the unfilled Back Bay, and the Worcester line from the west through Brighton and also via a causeway across the Back Bay.

In addition to these three railroads and the Eastern Railroad, four more railroads built lines into Boston during the 1840s and 1850s. All these, save one, established their terminals at the periphery of the built-up area. The exception was the Boston & Maine, which began servicing Boston in 1845 through a terminal at Haymarket Square. This line entered Boston from the north over a bridge across the Charles River. Between the end of the bridge at Causeway Road and Haymarket Square the line ran through a built-up area. While the citizens of Boston permitted the Boston & Maine to lay tracks through their city, they would not change the city ordinance which decreed that steam engines could not operate south of Causeway Road, so that when the Boston & Maine started their service they had to use mules to pull their cars the last few hundred yards between the Causeway and the Haymarket. The railroad expected the city to yield after the service was established, but in the ensuing contest of wills the pollution- and safety-conscious citizens proved to be the stronger. Eventually the Boston & Maine, considering steam power superior to mule power, moved their terminal to Causeway Road, where to this day the line terminates its service.

The railroads greatly facilitated the land-fill operations, for they permitted the inexpensive hauling of fill from outside the area. Boston was no longer restricted to leveling the Trimountains to gain land – a fast disappearing resource – and filling the Peninsula's coves one by one. Instead, the city could now fill its tidal flats on a grandiose scale.

During the next half century, all coves were filled, the Back Bay was transformed from a tidal swamp to the city's best residential area, and the South Bay, or Gallow's Bay, between the Shawmut Peninsula and the Dorchester Neck – South Boston – saw its tidal flats turned into ship and rail yards, wharves and warehouses. Through these land-recovery operations Boston more than doubled its inner city land area from 783 acres in 1804, when the first filling operations began, to 1,929 acres by the end of the century. In the process the narrow, pear-shaped and craggy Shawmut Peninsula, tied to the mainland by a narrow, marshy isthmus, became a rounded piece of level, well-drained land surrounded on three sides by water without a neck or isthmus. Aided by the railroads, Boston, which once did not have enough usable land for a medium-sized walking city, created sufficient access to the mainland to expand henceforth like any other land-rich city. Filling of the tidal flats in Massachusetts Bay continues to this day. In recent years most filling operations have been in East Boston, to expand the airport which is built entirely on fill. As the airport needs more and longer runways, the Boston shore-line is pushed steadily deeper and deeper out to sea.

Most of the fill operations occurred at public expense, though in the early days some of the land-recovery operations were undertaken by private parties who held title to the mud-flats. The city, and in the case of the Back Bay the state, owned the new won land. Still under the prevailing market concepts, neither placed special controls on the use to which the new lands were put. The lots, except those reserved for public use, were auctioned as quickly as possible to assure further funds for filling operations. Whether the buyers built on the lots or held them for speculation was their affair, not the public's.

The railroads not only changed the physical shape of Boston, they were also a major factor in changing the city's economic outlook. With railroads radiating from Boston to the north, the west and the south, the city gained improved access to the inland markets and no longer had to rely primarily on its ocean and coastal trade. At the same time, the railroads gave access to the port of Boston for the commercial and manufacturing interests located in the interior of the fast-growing United States. Though the railroads made the port of Boston more accessible, it never achieved the access to the interior that the port of New York enjoyed, first through the Hudson River, then the Erie

Canal and finally the railroads. Nonetheless, Boston's improved access was sufficient to stop the rate of erosion of its economic position compared to the other Atlantic seaports. Boston began to fall behind at the time of the inland canals construction in the early nineteenth century. The better inland access of these other major Atlantic ports apparently outweighed the fact that Boston is closer to Europe, Africa and the east coast of South America. Prior to the Panama Canal, Boston also had a distance advantage in trade with the west coast of South America and Asia.

The slow growth of the port of Boston in the early nineteenth century led Boston's capitalists to seek other investment opportunities. They found these in manufacturing. The rivers around Boston and generally throughout New England are not suitable for navigation, though their many rapids and falls make them an excellent source for cheap and reliable waterfall power. With the coming of the railroads, manufacturing plants could locate wherever there was water power, with less concern about locally available raw materials and local markets for the manufactured goods. By 1850 a whole string of such manufacturing towns had sprung up within one hundred miles of Boston. To the west there were Waltham, Fitchburg, Worcester, Chicopee and Pittsfield. To the northwest along the Merrimac River there were Lowell and Lawrence in Massachusetts, and Nashua and Manchester in New Hampshire. These towns had populations from 5,000 to 30,000 and were growing at a rate faster than the city of Boston.

Up to 1850, the population influx into these smaller towns came mainly from the surrounding farms, but Boston and the region as a whole could not have sustained this growth in industrialization without Irish immigrants. There were 115,000 in Massachusetts by 1850. In the words of Oscar Handlin's classical study, *Boston's Immigrants*:

Therein lay the significance of the Irish in the city's economic life. Before their arrival the rigid labor supply had made industrialization impossible. It was the vital function of the Irish to thaw out the rigidity of the system. Their labor achieved the transition from the earlier commercial to the later industrial organization of the city.[2]

The steam railroads, water power, immigration and the general industrial revolution, with its ever greater mechanization of the pro-

2. Oscar Handlin, *Boston's Immigrants*, revised and enlarged edn, Belknap Press of Harvard University Press, Cambridge, Mass., 1959, page 82.

duction process, had turned Boston during the first half of the nineteenth century from a commercial center to a city where industry and commerce flourished side by side.

In 1850, the Boston metropolitan area stretched to about two miles from City Hall and comprised, besides the City of Boston, the communities of Charlestown and Cambridge to the north and Roxbury to the south. The area had a population of about 190,000. For its internal transportation it relied on walking and the ferries. Omnibus service had been introduced as early as 1826, but it was slow and expensive and had no perceptible effect on the structure of the city. Like all walking cities, Boston and its adjacent communities were arranged to minimize transportation. Working-class, middle-class and upper-class residences were close to one another and manufacturing and commercial facilities were found throughout the area, in Boston as well as in the adjoining communities.

Horse-drawn street railways began operating in the Boston area as early as 1852, and were the region's main public transit system until the early 1890s. The horsecar line, quite in contrast to the later electric streetcar lines, had little effect on extending the outer periphery of the built-up area. During the forty years of the horsecar lines, the built-up area grew in most directions by only a little over a mile, and in no direction by more than two miles, though the population nearly tripled. To absorb such a population influx the Boston area needed to extend its urban fringe less than other urban centers, since these are the years in which Boston as well as Cambridge and Charlestown gained considerable usable acreage from land-fill operations.

Although the horsecars were not a very effective means for extending the city, they were a major force in reorganizing the area. Lines were constructed in the built-up areas and operated at an effective speed of five to six miles an hour, slightly faster than a person could walk. Over short distances the time differentials between the two modes were inconsequential. Thus, at first the horsecars did not attract the commuters. Most people still lived within easy walking distance of work and could save on fare and get to work in about the same time by walking. The horsecars attracted primarily passengers with bundles and parcels, and people on special errands to a distant part of the urban area.

The horsecars were a means to knit the various sections of the area together and in the horsecar decades Boston's corporate limits achieved their greatest expansion through annexation. First came Roxbury, the town on the mainland end of the Neck which was annexed in 1868, to

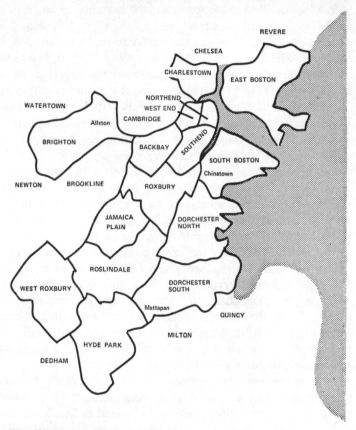

Map 3. *The districts of the city of Boston*

be followed by Dorchester across the South Bay in 1870. In 1874, Boston reached across the Charles River to annex Charlestown, and across the Back Bay to annex Brighton. That year, West Roxbury, the town to the southwest of Roxbury, also joined Boston's corporate limits. Since the horsecar era only one other town has been annexed to Boston – Hyde Park, in 1912.

Though the horsecars did not begin as commuter lines, in time they did attract commuters, who were generally of three types. First there were those who, under the influence of the horsecar, moved to the urban fringe and had to commute over two miles to work. Secondly, there were the railroad commuters, who lived in the countrified towns, came to the city by railroad and used the horsecars for crosstown commuting from the stations. These latter were usually from the upper-income groups. Both groups were rather small and had only marginal impact on the urban structure. Not so the third group. These were the workers, who, since the coming of the horsecar, had accepted new jobs in other parts of the urban area and chose to commute by horsecar rather than move their families. To this group must be added the new settlers, who first located in a congenial neighborhood and then scoured the whole urban area in the search for jobs. The horsecars were thus a definite force in reorganizing the spatially undifferentiated walking city into well-defined geographic neighborhoods for ethnic and socio-economic groups. That the horsecars as a commuter system were necessary to form socio-economically distinct neighborhoods is illustrated by the fate of the South End and the Back Bay. Both areas were built on filled land. The South End, which is the widened neck between the Shawmut Peninsula and Roxbury, was developed first. This occurred in the 1850s, the very beginning of the horsecar era. The South End was planned by its developers as an upper-income neighborhood with stately town houses, but the plan was premature. In the absence of accessible places of employment, the South End never quite made it as an upper-class neighborhood in spite of its truly outstanding architecture. From a good residential area it quickly turned into a rooming house area. By the turn of the century it was one of Boston's worst slum sections. The Back Bay was also developed as a purely upper-income residential area without any readily accessible employment generators. But development did not begin until the late 1860s and by then horsecars made distinct socio-economic neighborhoods possible. The Back Bay area has preserved its character as an upper-income residential area to this date, though most who live there now are college students and singles rather than families.

The horsecars were an immediate financial success, and there was a scramble for state charters and city franchises almost as soon as the first car had completed its first run. The high-density population led to a high-density ridership all day long and the problems of commuter travel with their morning and evening peaks had not yet appeared. As in other cities, the need for state and city sanction as well as the need for financing led to all sorts of chicanery and a proliferation of lines beyond what the market could economically support. The competition was so fierce that in the downtown area, where different lines crossed the same intersection or shared the same tracks for part of the run, competing drivers would do anything and everything literally to halt the competition. These tricks included stalling in intersections and racing for switches. The combination of anarchy on the rails and over-competition of lines generated pressures to rationalize the market through consolidation of ownership. Of the seven companies chartered to serve the Roxbury, West Roxbury and Dorchester areas, only four ever actually operated and by 1873 only two were still operating. This was almost twenty years before the electrification of the streetcar lines. These merger movements continued until 1887, when Henry M. Whitney, a steamship operator and real-estate investor, formed a syndicate out of his small West End Street Railway and began to purchase stock in Boston's other five operating companies in anticipation of electrification. After he had bought up large amounts of stock, especially in the biggest line, the Metropolitan, he offered through an exchange of stocks and bonds to combine all the companies into one. Minority stockholders, either helpless or in anticipation of great profits, agreed to the merger.

The system Whitney put together was sizable and reflects how important the horsecar had become to the urban environment. In 1889, the last year before the electric streetcars would begin operating in Boston on a regular basis, the West End Street Railway operated 253 miles of track, had 1,841 cars and 7,728 horses, carried 104 million riders and ran 16.5 million car miles.[3] If the system operated its lines

3. From Henry I. Harriman, *Rapid Transit Problems and Solutions*, in *Fifty Years of Boston (1880–1930)*, A Memorial Volume, Boston Tercentenary Committee, 1932.

If one measures the WESR's performance by the indexes developed in Table 3 (p. 147), Boston in 1889 had a Transit Availability Index of 359 and a Transit Usage Index of 231.

on the average of eighteen hours a day, seven days a week, these figures imply that there was a streetcar about every six minutes on every line, and that every Bostonian including babes in arms took slightly over two round trips every week.

A side effect of the merger was that the newly formed company contained all the stock of the former companies, much of which was 'watered' in the process of political and financial trickery which had accompanied the growth of the horsecar companies. The paper value of the company which emerged on the eve of the electrified era bore little resemblance to the productive value of the company's physical assets. Despite the financially weak underpinnings, it continued to expand the system in a manner regarded by some as uneconomical. For example, Warner has written:

Whitney continued two historic policies of street railway management. First, he was more interested in increasing the total number of fares on his system than in watching the relationship of distance, cost, and fare per ride. He, like his fellow streetcar managers the state over, was so convinced that the key to profit lay in the endless expansion of the numbers of passengers that, with little regard to costs, he constantly expanded the service area of the West End. As a result, by 1900 the outer limits of Boston's electric railways lay at least six miles from the downtown.

Second, Whitney, like all horsecar managers before him, was an ardent believer in the five cent fare. Thus expansion of service took place without additional charge to the commuter. As crosstown lines were built, free-transfer points were added, so that the nickel fare was almost universal in 1900. During the 1870s and 1880s eight cents had been required for many transfer rides; two full fares had been required where riders moved to the cars of different companies.[4]

This criticism raises an interesting question. Why should Whitney, who demonstrated such business acumen in other areas, act from ritual in the area of the street railway? The answer is that he was a far sharper operator than a mere look at his behavior in street railway management would suggest. If that behavior is put in the context of his overall activities, which Warner himself points out included real-estate develop-

4. Sam B. Warner, Jr, *Street Car Suburbs, The Process of Growth in Boston, 1870–1900*, Harvard University Press and the MIT Press, Cambridge, Mass., 1962, page 26.

ment, then his behavior becomes economically rational. Whitney apparently saw the electric streetcar as a means of developing outlying real estate. If the motive was real-estate development, then the idea of keeping fares down and extending lines as far as possible was rational in a business sense.

That this was indeed the motive can be gleaned from the early history of the Boston subway. The first tunnel in the Boston subway, the Tremont Street tunnel, opened for service in 1897, the first in the entire western hemisphere. The tunnel was not a product of the 'free enterprise' system. Rather, it was constructed by the city. Before the city undertook construction, all potential private entrepreneurs, including Whitney, were offered the 'opportunity' to build the line. However, not one of them accepted the offer. The subway tunnels would involve considerable capital costs. More important, the lines would run through the already built-up downtown area. This left no opportunity to offset these costs through capital gains from the abutting real estate. These entrepreneurs saw their profits not in transportation but in real estate. Once the city had built the tunnels, they were leased below cost to a private group of operators, the Boston Elevated Company. With streetcar service firmly established to his real-estate holdings, Whitney leased his West End lines to the Boston Elevated Company. Thus, the operation of all of Boston's transit lines were merged under one company, which in its downtown operation was greatly aided by the public investment in subway tunnels.

The new group of operators soon learned, what apparently Whitney already knew, there was no profit in transit operations, especially as the riders became predominantly commuters. The system that had served Boston adequately in 1900 could not accommodate the growing transport requirements of the next two decades, during which the population of Boston grew by 30 per cent and the surrounding communities by better than 50 per cent. Despite strong growth in ridership, the company never managed to show a profit, and by 1918 was bankrupt. This was at least in part due to their 1897 charter, which required the system to maintain the five cents fare with free transfers for at least twenty-five years.

Since transit was vital to the community and the private owners pleaded inability to improve operations, the Massachusetts State Legislature stepped in. A Public Control Act was passed. This Act assured continuance of transit service to the fourteen cities and towns which the Boston Elevated had serviced. The Act provided for continuation of operation of the transit system by the company, but now under the full operational control of a publicly appointed Board of Trustees, which had the right to set fares. The Act further provided for guaranteed annual returns of 5 to 6 per cent to the holders of the much-watered stock and the issuing of preferred stock for capital expenditure.

The Act finally provided that any excess profits would flow into a reserve fund the legislature had set up, and any deficit would be charged against this fund. If the monies in the fund fell below a set level, the property tax base of the fourteen cities and towns would be assessed for additional monies in proportion to the share of passenger traffic each community generated.

The 1918 Public Control Act was sold to the public as a temporary measure to get the Boston Elevated Company over 'momentary' financial difficulties. Naturally, this was not the case, and in spite of various reorganizations and an immediate doubling of the fare to ten cents, the transit system was never again to be privately operated.

History had repeated itself. Seventy years earlier the developers of East Boston found that once they had developed their real-estate holdings there was no incentive to operate a ferry that was not a money maker. Consequently, they dropped it on the taxpayers of Boston. So too in the era of streetcar development. Once the real estate had been developed, all objections to 'socialization' of the transport system disappeared.

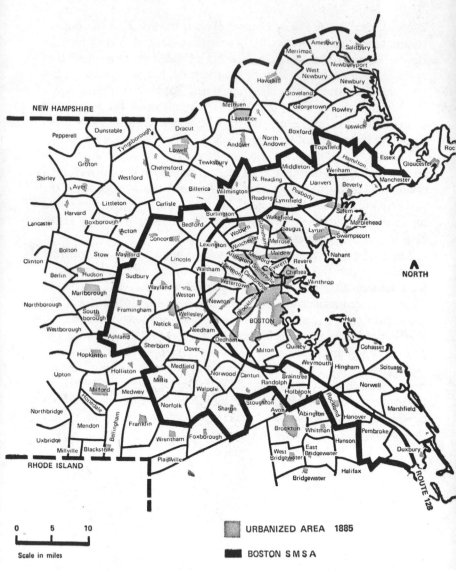

NEW HAMPSHIRE

RHODE ISLAND

NORTH

| 0 | 5 | 10 |

Scale in miles

▨ URBANIZED AREA 1885

▰ BOSTON S M S A

Map 4. *Boston urbanized 1885* (*data from* Boston Regional Survey, *Commonwealth of Massachusetts Mass Transportation Commission, 1963, Map 8*

Map 5. *Boston urbanized 1900 (data from* Boston Regional Survey, Commonwealth of Massachusetts Mass Transportation Commission, *1963, Map 34; covers only the inner 15–20 miles)*

NEW HAMPSHIRE

RHODE ISLAND

NORTH

Scale in miles

0   5   10

URBANIZED AREA   1960

BOSTON S M S A

Map 6. *Boston urbanized 1960* (*data from* Boston Regional Survey, *Commonwealth of Massachusetts Mass Transportation Commission, 1963, Map 8*)

NEW HAMPSHIRE

NORTH

RHODE ISLAND

▓ URBANIZED AREA 1970

■ BOSTON S M S A

5   10

Scale in miles

Map 7. *Boston urbanized 1970 (source: 1970 U.S. Census; covers the urbanized areas in the Boston, Brockton, Lowell and Lawrence-Haverhill Mass. portion, SMSA)*

CHAPTER 6

The Market City in the Automobile Era

Trucks, earlier than cars, changed the structure of the market-oriented Boston metropolitan area. In Boston, as elsewhere, there were passenger cars before there were trucks, and car registration always exceeded truck registration. Still, it was the truck's displacement of the horse-drawn dray that gave Bostonians the first inkling of the land-use changes the internal-combustion engine was going to generate in the decades to come.

Before the truck, industry had to locate in the urban core or at railroad sidings. Since these sites were limited, good industrial land was scarce. With truck transport any area with serviceable roads and not too far from the core could become an acceptable site. Trucks became generally available by 1909 and their impact on the metropolitan area was immediate (Table 2). Between 1909 and 1919 manufacturing employment in the inner-ring communities, two to six miles from the city center, grew dramatically faster than either closer in or further out from the center.

The shift to the inner-ring communities did not occur equally among all industries, but was concentrated in the 'high-value-added' industries. These are the industries that use relatively larger amounts of machinery, or capital, per worker, and that found it to their particular economic advantage to substitute truck shipment costs for high land prices. From 1914 on, the inner-ring communities outstripped the core in value added per production worker. The data suggest that some of the high-value added plants may have relocated from the outer-ring communities and the rest of Eastern Massachusetts, where they had rail access to Boston, to the inner-ring communities, where they depended on truck access. The 1920s, the second decade of the truck, were declining years for manufacturing employment in the Boston area. But this decline affected the inner-ring communities less than the core communities or those further out from Boston.

Table 2: Industrial growth in Eastern Massachusetts 1909 to 1929

	Index of production workers (1909 = 100)				Value added per production worker per annum[1]			
	1909	1914	1919	1929	1909	1914	1919	1929
Core communities (0–2 miles from the center of Boston)	100	107	119	101	$1,543	3,435	6,832	4,141
Inner-ring communities (2–6 miles)	100	108	152	133	$1,320	4,165	7,094	4,680
Outer-ring communities (6–12 miles)[2]	100	98	118	92	$1,002	2,721	5,479	3,117
Rest of Eastern Massachusetts	100	104	116	80	$1,016	2,453	5,508	2,432
	100	99	141	92	$1,090	2,656	4,993	3,154

1. This is the difference between the value of a firm's products and the cost of material, containers for products, fuel and purchased electric energy divided by the average number of wage earners for the year.

2. The data excludes Quincy which is dominated by a shipyard that grew rapidly during the First World War and just as rapidly declined. If Quincy is included in the outer-ring communities their data reads:

Data Source: U.S. Census of Manufacturing.

Between 1890 and 1910 the streetcars had expanded the built-up Boston area to include the residential neighborhoods of the inner-ring communities. The truck in the 1910s brought the economic base of the region into closer conformity with the residential patterns created by the trolley. With this shift in economic activity, it did not take public officials long to notice what was happening to their highways. A 1918 report of the Massachusetts Highway Commission noted that truck traffic was 'increasing much more rapidly' than auto traffic, the traffic the general public was talking about. By 1920, Massachusetts had 50,000 trucks, roughly one truck for every four cars, or a higher ratio of trucks to cars than at any time before or since. At the same time horse-drawn wagon traffic was falling off dramatically. The early shift to truck traffic and the official awareness of it partially explains why Massachusetts was one of the first states to have all its highways paved.

At the same time as the truck was bringing about closer spatial conformity between the residential and the industrial extension of the city, the automobile was repeating the feat of the trolley. It was dispersing the residential patterns beyond the area of economic activity. It was in the 1920s that the first beginnings of the automobile-based suburbanization occurred, but this suburbanization was still quite different from the one that followed the Second World War. Though the suburbanization of the inter-war years made allowances for auto access, it was still fundamentally public-transport based. All houses had driveways and frequently garages to provide off-street parking, and one-family homes became the rule rather than duplexes and triplexes; still the suburbanization occurred only where there was good access to Boston by public transit. The developers generally kept the lots sufficiently small to generate a traffic density that could support public transit – if everybody used it. The communities that experienced the greatest inter-war residential growth were the suburbs in the outer ring which in the days of the tracked city had formed the points of the star. During the 1920s, population growth ranged from 50 per cent in such southern and southwestern communities as Quincy, Braintree and Needham, to over 80 per cent in the western community of Wellesley, and over 90 per cent in the northwestern towns of Arlington and Belmont. Before the 1920s, suburban real estate had to locate within easy walking distance of either the railroad or public-transit facilities. In the 1920s, the automobile allowed the developer to move further away from the terminals. This brought additional land into the housing market and dropped accessible land prices sufficiently to expand the market for suburban living.

During the inter-war period, particularly during the depression years of the 1930s, Boston, like many other major North American metropolitan areas, constructed a system of 'parkways', that is landscaped roads that are restricted to 'pleasure vehicles'. While the depression decade is generally thought of as a time when little metropolitan change occurred, it was really the period that laid many foundations for the massive automobile suburbanization of the post-Second World War period. To combat the depression, local and federal monies were spent on public works projects, especially those that could be planned quickly and required many workers. Highways met this bill, if they could be planned quickly. In the Boston metropolitan area two governmental groups can build highways. First there is the State Highway Department, which in Massachusetts is known as the Department of Public Works (DPW). This group can build highways anywhere within the state after it acquires the land, either on the open market or through eminent domain, a time-consuming process. The other group is the Metropolitan District Commission (MDC), which through its park district can build parkways for 'pleasure vehicles' on its park land, which is located in thirty-six cities and towns of the Greater Boston area. Since the MDC owned its land already it could start construction projects quicker than the DPW. Thus it was the MDC which built most of the roads in the Boston area during the 1930s. By taking full advantage of all the available resources to combat the depression, the MDC built a network of roads and parkways that interconnected park and recreational areas and provided access to these from the population centers of the region. The road network has been modified over the intervening years, and today there are approximately 200 miles of so-called parkways under the control of the MDC.

The MDC's parks and parkways are one of those ironies of history when cities cause themselves untold pains by yielding to short-run market forces and political compromises without any thought for tomorrow and the day after. When in the second half of the nineteenth century the great cities of Europe built their grand avenues and parks, the movement quite naturally spread to the Western Hemisphere and

Boston. The clamor for parks arrived in the Boston area at about the height of the draining and land-filling operations of the marshes and wetlands with which the entire Massachusetts Bay region is so over-abundantly endowed. The urban conservationists insisted that some of these new lands be turned into parks. The city fathers of Boston and the surrounding towns could not neglect these desires, but as prudent businessmen they were not ready to turn over the best of the new land treasures to recreation and esthetics, rather than to tax-producing developments. A compromise was struck. The conservationists would get their parks, but not the square and rectangular expanses a park requires to be useful as a picnic, sports and play area, as well as for walks and carriage rides. The park land the city fathers set aside was the otherwise nearly useless banks of the numerous rivers and creeks that drain the area. Thus today the Boston area is full of parks, all administered by the MDC, and all but one – Franklin Park – long narrow strips of land. These strip parks were never able to provide Boston and the surrounding communities with the effective recreational facilities of Central Park in New York or Prospect Park in Brooklyn. The reason was not for lack of the designer's skill, for most of the Boston parks just as Central Park and Prospect Park, were the work of the great landscape architect Frederick Law Olmstead.

From the very beginning Boston's strip parks became favored targets for road builders. Olmstead's original designs had more roads than his square and rectangular parks. Still, there were Bostonians who recognized that roadways in these strip parks could quickly kill access to the water's edge, their greatest if not only recreational value. One leader in this road opposition was James Storrow, whose group in 1903 managed effectively to block a road along the Boston bank of the Charles River. In the 1930s, his widow made a generous gift for improvement and expansion of the Charles River front. The district accepted the gift, improved the parkland along the river and in addition built the roadway – now a four-lane parkway – her husband had fought thirty years before. But who could deny the husband his due – the river-front parkway is known to every Bostonian as Storrow Drive, and as a well-congested road during every morning and evening rush hour.

Because Storrow Drive is so busy, the MDC built pedestrian bridges across it, which permit those who can climb stairs safe access to the river front on all of six places over a distance of 9,000 feet. But there are hardly any bridges that cross the other MDC roads through the strip parks. Thus these roads have become effective barriers, for all but the most quick footed, between the built-up residential and commercial area and the little bit of green belt that fronts the waterways.

The short-run market had first forced the parks to be elongated strips of land basically unsuitable as recreational areas. Then the need during the depression to spend public works money quickly, forced roads through them, which killed most of their remaining recreational value and created an important ingredient for the massive suburbanization of the post-Second World War era.

The pre-Second World War transport studies of the Boston region show that, while there was a desire to expand the highway network of the region, public transport was still regarded as the prime mode for work trips and of importance for all other trip purposes as well. Thus, during the inter-war period four short extensions to the rapid transit lines were built. Given the poor financial condition of the system, these expansions did not extend the system at the fringes, but attempted to improve and maintain service in the previously built-up area. Thus it was by default that fringe development had to occur around the automobile.

The time between the wars also witnessed Boston's only closing of a rapid transit link. In 1938 the line running along Boston's waterfront between the two main rail stations, North Station and South Station, was closed. This line served as a link not only between the two terminals, but also between Boston's other transit lines and the port facilities on the Shawmut Peninsula and the East Boston Ferry. Ridership on the line had never lived up to expectation, at least in part because of the general decline of the port facilities on the Shawmut Peninsula. After the Sumner Tunnel opened in 1934 linking East Boston to Boston for automobile travel, and the municipally supported ferry closed, traffic on the line fell off even further and closing became the only apparent economic solution.

The inter-war years are the years in which Boston passed through its transportation balance between private and public travel modes. But, as elsewhere, it was not a stable balance – the pressure for more auto transportation was too strong. Within a month of the end of the

Second World War, the Department of Public Works initiated an official study the purpose of which was to gather information for planning highway construction throughout the state of Massachusetts. The result was the *Master Highway Plan*, publicly released in 1948. This plan marked the first official articulation of the view that private automobiles and not transit should become the primary travel mode of the region. The plan conceived of the region's highway system as a series of three circumferential roads connected by radials. The keystone of that system was and is the middle circumferential, Route 128. This road was pushed with such speed that the first miles were opened in 1947, even before the master plan was released. Route 128 runs around the Boston area approximately twelve miles from the center of Boston. The outer circumferential, Route 495, runs the same course, but at a distance of about twenty miles from the center, and was built during the sixties. The third circumferential, Route 295 or the Inner Belt, was designed to run within one to two miles of the very center of Boston's core. This third road, with the exception of one link, has never made it off the drawing boards.

At the time Route 128 was built it was a unique undertaking. The road was the first limited-access circumferential highway constructed around any major metropolitan area. It was not built to meet demand. Neither available traffic counts nor any reasonable extrapolation from them could have justified construction of the road at the time work on it began. Rather Route 128 was built to make the automobile the area's primary travel mode. Thus it was built not only as a bypass around the metropolitan area but also to supply and stimulate quick and easy access among Boston's far-flung suburbs, something a net of Boston-centered transit lines could never accomplish. Except for one minor section, the road was built – following the example of the German Autobahnen of the 1930s – to full limited-access standards. These standards require that the road be a divided highway, that no businesses or residences abut the road directly, that cars enter and leave the road only at designated interchanges, and that traffic does not cross the road at grade level, but is instead separated by bridges. Had there been unrestricted access to Route 128, that is, had the route been an arterial street, it would have quickly generated a large number of traffic-congesting roadside uses such as gas stations, hot-dog stands, car dealerships and discount houses; traffic speeds along the route would have dropped overtime to such an extent that the advantages as a time saver of the automobile over transit would have been far less significant.

While limited-access highways are very efficient as private car and truck roadways, they are severely deficient as local bus transit roadways. Local bus transit must get to the travelers' origin and destination, and these are never on the limited-access highways, but by definition on another local street. Thus, for public bus transit, arterial roadways, which have abutting origins and destinations, are superior to limited-access roadways. Route 128's design not only provided a positive means to turn the Boston suburban region over to the automobile, but it also created an effective barrier to the development of circumferential local bus transit.

Route 128 more than met its planners' and designers' expectations. It attracted traffic and centered all developments in suburban Boston around the automobile. In fact its very success soon became a problem. The original road was built with four traffic lanes, two in each direction. Before the completion of the last section in 1960, it had already become necessary to widen the older sections from four to six and even eight lanes. These widening operations required the tearing down and rebuilding of most bridges, which frequently were less than ten years old, for no one in the later 1940s had dared to authorize the expense of building bridges for future expansion of a road which no forecasted demand could justify. Where possibly could the traffic come from?

The traffic came from everywhere! It came from people who went only one and two interchanges along the route to go shopping, see friends, take care of personal business or go to work. It came from trucks and cars that traveled up and down the Atlantic Coast and wanted to bypass Boston. It came from traffic that needed access to one of the major arterials into the core area. It came from trucks that distributed their loads throughout the metropolitan area. In recent years more and more traffic comes from local residents who have found that the road enables them to accept new jobs thirty and fifty miles away, in and outside the metropolitan area, without changing residence. Route 128 traffic is not directional, but at all times carries more or less the same amount of traffic clockwise and counterclockwise around the Boston area.

Route 128 traffic grew and grew and still is growing because Boston's outer suburbs are growing. After fifteen years of depression and war, the late 1940s and 1950s saw an unprecedented housing boom. The housing boom naturally gravitated toward the automobile-based suburbs. Many factors contributed to this. The federal programs of low-cost mortgage loans financially enabled more people to become home owners. Automobiles with automatic transmissions made the automobile-based suburbs physically far more accessible. Land in the suburbs was cheaper, so lots could be larger or home prices lower. Finally, the air was cleaner. Home heating was converting from coal to gas and oil. The new residences in the suburbs all used the cleaner fuels while in the city most dwellings in any neighborhood still used coal.

Between 1940 and 1959, roughly 200,000 units were added to the housing market in the Boston Standard Metropolitan Statistical Area. Of these new housing units only 16 per cent were built in the city of Boston and an additional 20 per cent in the other cities and towns of the transit district. The other 64 per cent, or over 125,000 units, were built in the suburbs outside the transit district, primarily in communities which had no major highway or rail connection to Boston. In spite of the urban renewal efforts this trend is continuing. During the 1960s, Boston accounted for only 11 per cent of all new housing units, while the suburbs beyond the old transit district built 72 per cent of the new housing. This percentage is really an understatement, for the most active building in Eastern Massachusetts during the 1960s occurred generally in communities beyond the area that is officially known as the Boston S M S A.

Since there are paved roads everywhere, the development of automobile-based suburbs does not follow any particular highway or other road net patterns. The fact that one suburb grows faster than its neighbor is no longer a matter of transportation access – with the ubiquitous automobile access exists everywhere – but rather one of local policy. A community can effectively control its growth through zoning ordinances and building permits. The automobile-based suburbs of Boston present the same smorgasbord as those around Philadelphia, Los Angeles and other major cities. Just outside Route 128 and next to each other are the towns of Bedford and Lincoln. Both towns cover about 14 square miles in area. Both were originally farm towns with a population between 1,000 and 1,500. Both have direct rail access to Boston, and both towns attracted a few hardy commuters in the interwar years who wanted to live in the country. By 1940 Bedford had a population of 3,800, Lincoln was half the size. The willingness to be part of the metropolitan scene has always exemplified Bedford, while Lincoln steadily opted for the solitude of the rural atmosphere. Thus, even though Lincoln has the better road access to Boston and Cambridge and the more frequent rail service, Bedford has consistently outscored Lincoln in population and industrial growth. By 1965, Bedford had a population of over 10,000 and a higher employment to population ratio than even the City of Boston. Meanwhile, Lincoln had a population of just 4,400, and one of the lowest employment to population ratios in the metropolitan area, a ratio about one-tenth that of Bedford. Few can afford the luxury of Lincoln's rural solitude, thus the town's population has higher family incomes, lower fertility rates and more years of schooling than the residents of neighboring Bedford.

While the differences between other adjacent metropolitan towns may be less extreme, differences exist everywhere. In the automobile age these differences are no longer a function of transportation access, for auto access exists throughout the metropolitan area. In Boston this development was first aided by the parkways, which frequently are more convenient for inter-suburb travel than suburb–downtown travel, and of course by Route 128.

Since Route 128's overabundant traffic so clearly speaks for its transportation success, it is often credited with having generated the postwar economic growth that occurred in its environs. There is a popular myth which argues that the building of the road caused the hightechnology electronics industry to locate in the areas around the road. Thus it is reasoned by analogy if other areas built similar roads, they could expect similar economic booms. The location of the electronics industry and the road in about the same place was not cause and effect, it was a simultaneous occurrence. The highway engineers picked the location because they wanted to locate the road as close to the metropolitan area as possible to maximize its traffic volume, and at the same time locate it far enough from the center to minimize the land-taking problems and costs. The ideal site was thus the first open stretch beyond the built-up portion of the metropolitan area.

During the years the road was being built, the electronics industry across the nation began to burgeon. Since the Massachusetts Institute of Technology (MIT) in Cambridge, across the Charles River from Boston, had always been in the forefront of electronics research, numerous electronics firms began to arise in its environs, just as other electronics companies clustered around Stanford University on the San Francisco Peninsula. The new companies around MIT needed land to build their facilities and more often than not chose acreage in the first open spaces beyond Cambridge. This open land was in several communities: Waltham, Lincoln, Bedford, Lexington, Burlington and Wilmington. Electronics firms sprang up on properties in all these communities within ten to fifteen miles of one another. Since these companies rely on a common labor pool and bravely steal each other's engineers and technicians, a common name was needed, and what better name was there than the '128 industries'. It was the birth of this name that gave rise to the legend that the highway, rather than the availability of open land and the proximity to MIT, was the cause for the industry to locate where it did.

If the area had had a different name no one would have confused the growth of the industry with the location of the highway. The electronics industry on the San Francisco Peninsula which clusters around Stanford University is not known as the 'Bayshore' industry, even though its plants are closer to the Bayshore Freeway than the Boston plants to Route 128. Lacking nominal identification, no one is foolish enough to credit that freeway with this industrial growth.

Had Route 128 truly been the attraction, Boston's electronics firms would have located much closer to it than they did. Many plants, and especially the older ones, are three to five miles from the highway. Had management truly thought in terms of the bypass rather than access to Cambridge, the industry would have arisen all along Route 128, to the north and to the south of Boston, rather than in the one narrow northwest sector that is bound by the old highways and commuter railroads that lead out from Boston through Cambridge. The industry which Route 128 actually did attract was not the glamorous electronics firms, but the more mundane warehouses which moved here from the inner city. By having their trucks and shippers use the circumferential high-way, these operators in effect could cut their distribution costs in the Boston metropolitan area.

The early construction and successful design of Route 128 led to its serving as a buffer permitting a slower rate of highway construction within the metropolitan area. Since it was easy to find land in the low-density regions beyond Route 128 for highway purposes, the construction of roads into the Boston area as far as Route 128 proceeded quite rapidly, as the circumferential route provided a fine natural terminus until construction on the inside could begin. As a consequence, the outward portions of Routes 1, 2, 24, I-93 and the Massachusetts Turn-pike were completed as far as Route 128 during the 1950s and early 1960s. Until 1959, the only two major automobile facilities completed within Route 128 were the Southeast Expressway and the Tobin Bridge to the North Shore.

With the post-war era came a major shift in highway financing. Until the Second World War, highway construction and maintenance in the United States was usually financed from general tax revenues, and appropriations for highways had to compete with the financial require-ments of other government services. This had been in the interest of the highway lobbies, since road construction and maintenance funds exceeded the funds collected from the gasoline and other automobile-related taxes. By the 1940s, all roads had been drained and graveled and all highways paved. Year-round automobile travel was possible everywhere. Future road construction funds were not needed to build a basic automobile road network, but only to improve the network with bigger, better and safer roads. If need be, road expenditure could be decreased for other more urgent public needs. Meanwhile with in-creased auto travel the tax revenues from automobile usage were climb-ing and by the late 1930s and 1940s were generally larger than the necessary expenditures for road maintenance and minimal road con-struction. Motor vehicle traffic could now generate tax revenues for other government functions. To assure the further development of the highway net, regardless of other public needs, this 'diversion' of automobile-related taxes to other than highway-related uses had to be prevented. The highway interests thus began to push in state after state for so-called 'anti-diversion' provisions. These provisions earmarked all taxes generated by motor-vehicle usage exclusively for highway-related uses. In Massachusetts, the 'anti-diversion' provisions became part of the state's constitution in 1948. By this method the necessary state funds were guaranteed for Route 128 and other new highway improvements throughout the state.

On the federal level, an informal linkage between road-user-generated taxes and reimbursements to the states for highway costs had been in effect since 1934. This practice was frozen into law in 1956 when the federal gasoline taxes were sharply increased and the National Highway Trust Fund was set up. This fund, as the general appropriations before, provided up to 50 per cent reimbursement to the states for the construction of primary and secondary roads, and in addition 90 per cent reimbursement for the building of a new national limited-access highway net, the 'National System of Interstate and Defense Highways', or for short the Interstate System. This road network is 41,000 miles in length and contains 5,000 miles of roadway in urban areas. The Eastern Massachusetts portion of the network is 195 miles long. The target date for the completion of the Interstate Highway System is 1975.

With this new federal largess and the protected state highway funds, highway construction could go into high gear unfazed by any other demands for public monies from public transit, for education, national defense, health and welfare. In the five years before Boston's monumental traffic jam of 1963, fifty miles of brand-new highway construction was completed in the region. While these programs assured ample monies for highway construction, no funds were allocated to expand parking. Indeed, it was actively discouraged. Beginning in 1956 the state made virtually no-strings-attached highway aid available to the cities and towns. The only limit placed on this highway money was the expressed statutory prohibition on using the money to extend or maintain off-street parking facilities.

The expansion of highway facilities after the Second World War meant that the transport balance struck during the inter-war years was utterly shattered. The post-war era was one in which public transport floundered badly. At the close of the war a study commission looked into Boston's public transportation picture and concluded that the only solution to the acute financial problems and chronic deficits (which abated only during the war years) was public ownership. From 1918 until 1947 the lines were publicly administered but privately owned. In 1947 the Metropolitan Transit Authority (MTA) was formed to purchase the lines and equipment of the Boston Elevated. It then became the provider of public transportation service in the fourteen cities and towns formerly served by the 'El'. Public ownership proved to be an illusory panacea. The deficits between 1947 and 1963 continued to grow worse and worse. The problem was not so much one of management and ownership as of marketplace economics. The growth in the region was dominated by the highways and as a consequence transit patronage fell off.

During this period the most significant improvement to transit service occurred in 1959, the year the 9.4 mile Riverside extension was placed into service. The line was built on an abandoned railroad right-of-way which was free of street crossings at grade level. With this extension transit service was now available from downtown towards the west as far out as Route 128 to an area just south of the region where the electronics industry located and north of the warehouse region. Despite this mislocation, traffic on the line more than justified its development almost from the very beginning, not as a hauler of workers to Route 128, but as a carrier of traffic into central Boston. A second expansion of the system was less successful. In the early fifties the East Boston Line was extended past Logan International Airport into the city of Revere. This line never lived up to expectations in terms of commuter passenger traffic because it competed not only with automobiles able to reach Boston from the north over the newly opened Tobin Bridge and through the Sumner Tunnel, but also with commuter trains and bus lines running directly from the major North Shore population centers into downtown Boston. The line is unique however, since it was the first attempt to provide rapid transit service to a major airport.

While the expansion of service was getting mixed reviews, the financial condition of the MTA was consistently bad. This poor financial health contributed to the replacement of streetcar service with bus service, the substitution of a less-comfortable for a more comfortable service. Bus service has two advantages to transit administrators which outweigh the comfort loss to passengers. First, buses are flexible in terms of routes, an important quality when you are attempting to follow the needs of your passengers. Secondly, the purchase price of buses is lower than that of streetcars or rapid-transit cars. While the switch to buses allowed more flexibility and lower equipment costs, the higher operating and depreciation costs of this mode become a greater problem as time passes.

If the massive traffic jam of 1963 was the result of the convergence of a number of extraordinary factors alone, little more needs to be said. However, in retrospect it is apparent that those responsible for the various uncoordinated parts of metropolitan Boston's transport system could not have consciously designed a better overall strategy for disaster. Their plans generated large sums of money for highway construction; no or very little money for public parking, especially in the inner-core area; and no funds for public transport other than a minimal subsidy to slow the rate of deterioration in service levels. Even this minimal subsidy was paid from a regressive source, a tax levy upon real estate in the inner-core region. What design could better concentrate cars in the metropolitan area and wait for the right set of events to set off a massive traffic jam!

The 1963 traffic jam served as a catalyst to move those concerned about the various aspects of transport to quicker action. In response to the need to get more cars off the streets, 10,000 new off-street parking spaces were built in the City of Boston between 1965 and 1968 alone. More highways were built in hopes of easing the seemingly endless problem of automobiles. One of the most important of these roads was the extension of the Massachusetts Turnpike, a toll road, from its previous terminal at Route 128 all the way into downtown Boston. This new extension was opened in 1965. This road was crucial to insure that a repetition of the 1963 disaster would not occur. It became, in effect, a safety valve. The turnpike charges a rather stiff toll for the eleven miles from Route 128 to downtown Boston. This 55 cent toll acts to keep that section of road underutilized in even severe rush-hour traffic. However, at times when traffic begins to build up on other radials, the turnpike extension can pick up the surplus and move it out to Route 128, where it can be distributed over the circumferential highway.

The public transport officials, too, responded to the crisis. Since a major portion of the public transportation problem was the spiraling deficit between fare-box receipts and costs, a solution was sought to spread the costs over a larger area. It was hoped that by broadening the support base and lessening the burden of support upon the property-tax base of the fourteen inner-core communities, it would be possible to generate the level of funding necessary to upgrade the system. They argued that the public transport system serves not only the direct users in the fourteen cities and towns of the MTA district but all who benefit from a prosperous and healthy metropolitan area. Consequently, the support for the public transport system should come from the seventy-eight cities and towns which comprise the metropolitan area. In order to get the necessary political support for this increased tax burden from the outlying communities, it was necessary to provide some direct service to these communities. A new metropolitan-area-wide transport system was created. It not only served the inner core, but also took over public transport services in the outlying communities either by directly buying out existing companies or by providing subsidy to private operators and commuter railroads. This new agency, the Massachusetts Bay Transportation Authority (MBTA), came into existence on 1 January 1965.

This reorganization, as all previous ones, did not help much. Since the problem plaguing public transportation is the result of the more fundamental facts, such as the ever-growing automobile facilities and the resultant sprawl, the reorganization could not stop the continued upward spiral of the deficits. Indeed the period of the late sixties, with its inflationary pressures, began to push up the deficits still further. However, because the deficit was now being spread over more cities and towns, the region has delayed a financial crisis of sufficient severity to cause a disruption of service. Though all these actions bought time for the urban transportation in the metropolitan area, they did not halt the automobile-based exodus out of the regional core. Retail trade continued to move to the suburbs, as did the manufacturing industries. However, 1963 marked an important turnabout for Boston. Until then the trend in total jobs was downward. In that year, for the first time since the employment peak of 1947, jobs in the city began to move up. The increase was due to a job rise in the services, the government, and the real-estate, insurance and finance industries. However, the decline in trade and manufacturing continued. Part of the turnabout can be explained by the fact that the core was the natural area for those activities which operate at the interstices of the economy. Part of it is also explained by the growth of more high-rise housing and office development in the city. This effort was partly spontaneous and partly encouraged by the use of urban renewal funds and tax incentives.

The creation of more off-street parking, the opening of the Massachusetts Turnpike Extension into Boston and the reorganization and slight extension of the public transport system all were responses which attempt to make the status quo more livable. However, they were not the main transportation trend. This was to build more highways in more directions and more quickly. The building rush of 1958–63 was largely outside Route 128 because it takes longer to plan highway construction within a densely populated area. After 1963 the preliminary land-taking for the construction of highways inside Route 128 began to get underway in earnest, and land-taking on a grand scale it was. The standards for interstate highways are such that many valuable acres of prime land are swallowed up to create a single interchange. The planned Innerbelt-Southwest Expressway interchange required the taking of 479 structures and the displacing of 326 families. Yet unless the state builds roads which conform to these outlandish standards, they lose the lucrative 90 per cent federal reimbursement. In the Boston area, at about the same time that highway land-taking was getting underway, land-taking for many urban renewal projects was also occurring. The cost-benefit logic of highway construction leads the engineers to choose routes with the lowest land costs to maximize 'returns to society'. At the same time, urban renewal seeks to redevelop those areas which contribute least to the municipal tax base. Taken together these programs almost invariably chose the land which the lower and lower middle classes call home.

The result of these massive land-takings, which really began to be felt throughout the inner core of the metropolitan area in the winter of 1965–6, was to jolt the affected communities into organizing themselves to protect what was left of the homes and neighborhoods which they knew. And organize they did! The organization cut across ethnic lines. A coalition of groups from Irish, Italian, black, Chinese, Spanish and ethnically nondescript neighborhoods was able effectively to make common cause. These groups may have fought bitterly about schools and public services but they were united in their opposition to any more highway construction in their neighborhoods. No politician, with any thought about a future career, can counter this sort of opposition on sheer pragmatic grounds. In addition there was much logic and good sense in the positions these neighborhood coalitions were taking. This combination proved irresistible. Between demonstrations, negotiations, court orders and press conferences the coalition was able to delay virtually all construction, until finally in 1970 the Governor of Massachusetts ordered a moratorium on further highway construction inside the Route 128 area, with the exception of the I-93 freeway extension into downtown Boston, where the construction contracts had already been let. The moratorium would remain in effect until a major restudy of the region's transportation needs could be completed. The ability of the Governor to yield to the arguments and political pressures of the community groups was enhanced by the fact that the steps which had been taken between 1963 and 1966 to relieve the immediate pressures of traffic chaos were successful.

With the conclusion of the restudy in late 1972, the Governor announced a transportation plan which was based primarily on transit. The plan wiped out all previous plans for the Inner Belt freeway within two miles of downtown and three radial freeways between the Inner Belt and Route 128. There would be widening and upgrading of a few arterials, particularly in the northern sector, and the building of a new harbor crossing between downtown and the airport. This new harbor crossing, a two-lane tunnel, has a few previously unheard of features. First, the tunnel would be restricted to trucks and buses. Never before has there been a road from which the private automobile was excluded. Secondly, the new tunnel would be toll-free, while the other tunnels and the bridge would continue to charge tolls. Thus cars which want to enter the downtown area from the north and northeast would pay tolls, while trucks and buses would not. These features could make the tunnel, if built as specified, as important a transportation event as Route 128 was a quarter of a century ago. In the late 1960s, the wholesale produce market moved from the South Station area, just south of downtown, to Chelsea, north of the harbor. Chelsea is also the major distribution point for oil. With the free truck tunnel there may be further moves of the distribution industry to the areas on the north side of the harbor, creating space for the downtown office district to expand towards the south.

Besides this highway building, the plan proposes to extend the rail transit system along nine lines to Route 128 and build large parking lots at the end of these lines. The transit plan also proposes a circumferential transit line two miles from downtown, where twenty-five years ago the highway advocates planned the now defunct Inner Belt freeway.

The new transportation plan is courageous, and if implemented would do much to re-create a balanced transportation system to which all age groups have equal access, and which does not unduly favor the middle-age, middle-class group as a highway-oriented system does. But as the 1948 Master Plan was never completed, so one can confidently prophesy that the 1972 plan will not be implemented in its entirety. Planning is relatively simple, implementation takes money. The political storm against the new Master Plan by the pro-highway forces is just gathering momentum. Will Massachusetts and the nation really decide to allocate most of the urban transportation resources to public transportation rather than private highway transportation? Massachusetts needs federal funds to implement its new transportation plan. Even though it can be shown that public transportation makes more sense in dense urban areas than the continued expansion of highways, this will make little difference as long as massive resources are available for the highway alternative. Without a shift in resource allocation the demand for transportation will of necessity be filled through the available supply, even if it is more costly in the long run. Thus the future of Boston and other major cities depends upon the political decisions made in the nation's capital. On that front, the battle is just beginning.

CHAPTER 7

The Social Crisis

By now it is hardly news that the United States' major metropolitan areas, and even many of its minor ones, are in a state of crisis. While the extent of the problem may differ, the basic symptoms are the same everywhere. In spite of urban renewal, large areas of the cities are in a state of physical decay; slums are growing, not shrinking. The central cities and surrounding suburbs reel from waves of violence. Crime rates, particularly those for violent crimes, are shockingly high and generally rising. Drugs are common in the inner city as well as the most affluent suburbs. Alienation abounds. Increasingly, people feel that they are no longer master of their fate, that they are picked on and put upon, that they are buoyed about by forces they do not control, and that those in control do not understand their needs, hopes and desires. Meanwhile municipal services are deteriorating. Quite apart from public transit, neither the schools, the hospitals, the police, nor the garbage collectors represent the quality of service and responsiveness they used to. In reciting such a litany it makes little difference if one thinks of the older cities along the Eastern Seaboard, such as New York, Boston, Philadelphia or Baltimore; the industrial giants of the Midwest, such as Chicago, Detroit, Cleveland or St Louis; the newer metropolitan areas, which had most of their growth in the last thirty years, such as Los Angeles, Houston or Miami; or such smaller cities and their environs as Columbia, La Crosse or Nashua. The problems everywhere are more or less the same.

It is our contention that the urban crises which manifest themselves in so many different ways have at least one common root. This is the increasing reliance on the automobile. In every urban area the automobile has become the only means of transportation by which every part of the region can be reached. In addition, metropolitan activity and land-use patterns have become so dispersed that neither the automobile nor any public transit system can furnish the mobility required by every individual to function with reasonable ease in the activities their respective social, economic and physical well-being demands.

Wherever the automobile is *the* mode of travel, there access to transportation is distributed very unevenly among individuals. This is probably the greatest social fault of the automobile, though little has been said or written about the long-term consequences of this uneven access. The uneven access to transportation is also the most vital new factor which the automobile introduced into urban society. Before the automobile, access to transportation was very evenly distributed. As long as walking was the norm for urban movement, all but the lame had equal access to mobility. With tracked transportation, the fare created a difference in access, but this difference was minor compared to what the automobile has created.

There are many factors that account for the uneven access to automobility. Full automobility requires that a person can drive and has a car readily available. For most, these conditions are met infrequently or not at all. To drive legally, one needs a driver's license, and even in the United States nearly half the people (47 per cent) do not possess this document. Predominantly, these are the young and the old, but even in the age groups of 25 to 45 at least 10 per cent are without a driver's license.

Since the automobile has become *the* local transportation system, one would expect a national policy to make everyone a driver. But this is not the case. Quite to the contrary. The automobile is a deadly weapon in the hands of the unskilled, and in the name of highway safety there are active and effective policies to reduce the driving population by taking 'unsafe drivers off the road'. For example, there is the general policy of revoking drivers' licenses for frequent minor traffic violations as well as severe single traffic infractions. Quite often this means that a person is in effect legally prevented from going to work, shopping and generally taking care of personal business, unless a relative or friend who can drive is available, or taxi service and fare present no problem. It is no surprise that under these conditions many drive even though their licenses are revoked. Besides 'punishing' people for road infractions through license revocation, the restrictive policy is evident in the issuing of licenses. At one time most states issued licenses to 14- and 15-year olds; today the minimum driving age is at least 16, but often

16½, 17 and in some states even 18. Once driver's licenses were issued with minimal road tests or none at all. Today periodic eye tests are routine and many states are introducing periodic road tests. For young and middle-age drivers these tests are usually restricted to those who have been involved in traffic accidents or violations, but older drivers are forced to take them regularly on an annual or biannual basis.

As there are more cars on the road and highway travel becomes faster, drivers – for safety's sake – must have rather fast reflexes. Thus many drivers, long before they lose their licenses, voluntarily restrict their driving to local streets, avoid expressways, and often confine themselves to the daylight hours of light traffic. These restrictions, be they voluntary or legal sanction, limit the automobility of a large segment of the population.

Little concern has been expressed about the effects on the young and the elderly of the increased reliance on the automobile as *the* primary form of urban transportation. The common feeling is that nearly every family has a car and that, therefore, all members of the family have adequate mobility.

There are two fallacies in this assumption. First, not all families own cars. In 1971 in the United States, according to the U.S. Census, a little over a fifth (22 per cent) of all families living in metropolitan areas owned no car, and in the central cities nearly a third (32 per cent) of the households were carless. These percentages have not changed markedly in the last decade. The lack of ownership is greatest among the poor and aged. Nationally, over half (56 per cent) of those with income of less than $3,000 are carless, and nearly half (45 per cent) of the households with heads 65 years of age and older own no car. Since many of the aged are also poor, lack of income rather than advanced age might be expected to be the cause of the massive lack of car ownership in the older population. While this is certainly a factor, still income bracket by income bracket the ownership of cars in households with heads over 65 is significantly lower than for households with younger heads.

Transportation planners usually assume that a family with one car has all the required mobility. To have more than one car is a luxury, not a necessity. Though a family often can arrange to live with one car and no public transit, this arrangement may involve considerable hardships. Take the case of a rather typical suburban one-car family. If the husband has a job with regular hours and a regular place of work, he may be able to join a car pool, but this still means he must take the car once or twice a week. If he has irregular hours or reports here today, there tomorrow, he needs the car for work. Also, if the husband took his present job after locating the family, rather than vice versa, the chances are considerably better than even that the length of his journey to work increased from his previous employment. For instance, in the Boston area the 1969–71 recession, which hit the suburban industries particularly hard, brought with it a marked increase in rush-hour travel along Boston's circumferential highway. Since employment did not increase, the explanation seems to be longer work trips. Longer work trips usually make it more difficult to find car pools, especially if one works in suburbia. If the husband needs the family car to go to work, chances are the wife can work only if she can find employment while the husband is not at work, so that one car can seriously limit a family's income potential. Lansing and Hendricks[1] have shown that families with the same income but two or more workers are more likely to be multi-car owners than families with just one worker.

To combat congestion and to decrease the cost of commuting, car pools have long been a favored device of planners and economists. Most cars can carry five or six persons, rather than the usual one or two. If people would share rides, it is argued, present roads could carry two to three times the number of travelers during rush hours; parking requirements and pollution would be reduced; and generally the cost of transportation would be lower. The public, on the other hand, has held car pools in rather low esteem and has reverted to them only if required to by other family members' need for the car, high parking fees, or very long and strenuous commutes. Survey after survey has shown that automobile occupancy is lower for the journey to work than for any other type of journey. The results of the 1970 U.S. Census are revealing. Nationwide, only 16 workers commute as auto passengers for every 100 workers who commute as auto drivers. The ratio in the central cities is slightly larger than in the suburbs, since the ratio appears to be strongly determined by income. Thus the rural blacks,

1. John B. Lansing and Gary Hendricks, *Automobile Ownership and Residential Density*, Survey Research Center, The University of Michigan, Ann Arbor, Michigan, 1967.

generally a poverty group, have a significantly higher auto passenger ratio than any region, state or urban area. In this group there are 62 workers who commute as auto passengers for every 100 that drive. Meanwhile, in the most affluent suburban neighborhoods the ratio on the trip to work hovers around 8 auto passengers to every 100 drivers.

Car pools may be appealing in principle, but for the traveler they are more likely than not a nuisance. For a car pool to function smoothly, that is, without ruffling the feathers of its various members, each person must be picked up at precisely the agreed time, and each must be ready when the pool arrives. In the evening the pool must be ready to leave at the agreed time and nothing is more irritating than a car pool member who can't leave work on time. For all practical purposes, a car pool is a transit system with one round trip a day. There is no choice of departure time. A car pool chains one to a schedule. It may operate in a private car, but from the traveler's point of view it is not a personal car. In a car pool, as in any infrequently scheduled transportation system, the traveler queues up and waits for the vehicle to serve him; whereas the joy and convenience of the private auto is precisely the fact that it queues up and waits for you. It is prepared to serve you, the driver, any time you are ready.

If the family's one car is used for commuting, all other functions that require transportation must take place outside working hours. Suburbia's retail merchants recognize this fact, and stores regularly remain open evenings and all day Saturday. Over the years these have become the hours when the suburban supermarkets and stores are crowded.

The typical suburban youngsters below driving age have little independent mobility, but must rely on their parents to chauffeur them. In the one-car family they must wait until father is home from work so that he or mother can chauffeur them. This is by no means an idle observation but a fact that has become ingrained in the suburban travel patterns. The 1969 transportation study of the Northern Middlesex area,[2] one of Boston's suburban sectors, observed that auto passenger traffic peaked in the evening between 7 and 8 P.M. During this hour auto passenger traffic was 16 per cent higher than during the morning

2. Analytical Systems Corporation, *Transportation Demand Characteristics in the Northern Middlesex Area*, Interim Report No. 2 for the Northern Middlesex Area Commission, Lowell, Mass., October 1969.

rush hour. Much of this evening auto passenger traffic was generated by the 5- to 15-year age group. Since these youngsters needed to be chauffeured, the study found that during the same hours the 30- to 49-year-old drivers, presumably the parents, generated correspondingly heavy 'serving passenger' trips.

Finally, the one-car family is faced by another dilemma, if it must rely on a functioning car for all its transportation needs. There is no time to service or repair the car, if the car is needed for commuting during regular working hours. Such cars are tied up during the only hours the garages are open. With less competition than the retail stores, garages need not stay open evenings and weekends and these cars are maintained either badly by weekend mechanics or not at all. This poor maintenance is not just the owner's loss but generates increased ecological costs as well. Poorly maintained cars do not last as long; they are junked sooner, which creates increased automobile graveyard and recycling problems. Poorly maintained cars are also less safe, which can contribute to accidents. Finally, poorly maintained and tuned engines generate more air pollution.

Where the car is the only transportation mode, the one-car family operates a transportation system without a back-up. This also applies to the two-car family with two workers who both need a car. No bus company or airline would dare to buy just as many vehicles as their peak-hour operations require. All fleet operators expect some of their vehicles to be out of service and in the shop. But what family can afford an extra car, just so that the needed cars are always available? No one knows the hours and days that are lost from car owners' jobs because the old car won't start or has to be taken to the shop. Naturally, these losses hit hardest those who can least afford them, the ones with the lowest paying jobs and the oldest cars.

In a society where the car is the only available mode of transportation, limited access to the automobile will prevent many trips from being made. This applies even to the affluent. The young can leave their immediate neighborhood only if someone will chauffeur them. Modern youngsters cannot explore the urban area like the city kids of past generations who used the streetcars to travel far and wide. And considering that most neighborhoods, especially in suburbia, are rather uniform in their socio-economic status and the age of their residents this becomes a true loss. The children grow up with far less direct exposure to other age groups and to people of markedly different socio-economic circumstances than past generations. Neighborhoods housing nuclear families of parents and minor children generally have a deficiency of young adults and old people. The youngsters in such an environment are not exposed to the proverbial cranky old woman who chases them from her yard or front porch, or chides them for this or that little inconsequentiality. But while the irritants of extreme age groups meeting each other have been removed, so also has the natural educational process of learning to live with people who are unlike oneself or one's parents. The young and the old are not really enemies – many elderly thrive on visits and occasional encounters with the young, and the young likewise can be enthralled by the old and their tales of long ago. Finally, in moments of conflict at home, who can be better and wiser counselors than the grandparents, a child's natural enemies, or someone of similar age. These people have fought the battle of childhood, and of child rearing, and can counsel with the detachment that the lack of direct daily responsibility affords.

While the absence of the aged cheats the child of exposure to how other people live, the absence of young adults makes the neighborhood teenagers unusually cocksure of themselves. These teens see only adults to whom they do not relate and youngsters over whom they can lord. If young adults are present, a natural pecking order develops. Here for each child or teenager there is someone just a bit older and more mature, a natural big brother or sister.

Without the aged and young adults as mediators in the natural battle between the generations, such conflicts become easily exaggerated. The age-segregated neighborhood – which became a feasible urban form only when the automobile became commonplace – is a natural breeding ground for insecurity and alienation. The harassed child turns to rebellion, drugs and delinquency and the harassed parent to alcoholism and divorce. Naturally, the automobile-generated transportation and land-use patterns are not the sole cause of these pathologies, for most suburbanites are quite 'normal', but these patterns are contributory factors which help to explain the steady rise in the number of people who become victims of these pathologies.

Even if the children are chauffeured out of their immediate neighborhood, their destinations are limited. They can only go where their chauffeurs care to take them and only when they choose to do so. By being chauffeured to specific places, children more likely than not fail to see the seamy side of town, or the multitudinous events that present themselves to the strollers in urban neighborhoods where people still are more likely to walk than to ride. These places are not destinations of 'planned' trips. But even the destinations of 'planned' trips are more often than not beyond the child's reach. One father told us of his utter amazement when his son, who had just received his license, recited a litany of places where he could now go on his own. The places included secondhand book shops, libraries and stamp dealers – all locales the parents approved of, but which the parents, who had other predilections, only rarely cared to take their son to. Naturally, the boy was reluctant to ask to be taken, for who wants to go with a bored companion or receive a 'no' for one's quite legitimate request.

Many of today's younger parents were once themselves youngsters in auto-dependent and auto-limited suburbs, and may regard youth's lack of mobility as the 'norm' with no real effect on child development. But in the days past when mobility, and not its lack, were the norm, child development psychologists considered it an asset. A case in point are the writings of Dr Arnold Gesell and his colleagues at Yale University. These scientists did their research prior to the early 1950s. At that time they developed 'growth gradients', which describe a child's behavior at various age levels up to age 16. Between the ages of 8 and 14, the researchers used independent travel as the measure for a youth's facility to orient and master space. These are excerpts from their findings:

8 years: Can go to city on bus if put on and met by someone.

9 years: Can go to familiar places on bus, getting on alone; or go downtown alone.

10 years: Ten can often manage bus trips downtown. Some can do so if they are meeting an adult, others can go and return unaccompanied on simple errands, even going to the dentist alone. A few, however, are still not allowed to cross a busy street.

11 years: Can go downtown alone on the bus, even travel on the train, if they do not have to change trains.

12 years: Many now travel alone on the train, can find their way in strange cities asking policeman or others.

13 years: Now parents describe children as going to Boston and New York alone, rather than 'downtown' as at 10.

14 years: Many 14-year-olds travel independently now without difficulty.[3]

Gesell's gradients are known to represent slow-maturing rather than fast-maturing children. Thus most youngsters mastered independent travel at even earlier ages. A careful reading of the gradients shows little if any growth between 9 and 10. One possible explanation is that the gradients for 8 and 9 were published in 1946, but those for 10 and older in 1956. During the interval, the post-Second World War move to the suburbs got into full swing, together with a severe decline in public transportation.

By now the gradients are inapplicable to suburban youngsters. The vast majority have never been on any public vehicle. Their first solo excursions were probably by bicycle, but these vehicles transported them hardly further than the local school bus. Beyond this immediate area, their first solo excursion occurs more often than not at 16 or 17 after they have gotten their driver's license and are permitted to borrow the family car.

This late date of solo excursions beyond the immediate neighborhood may have some striking social consequences. Youngsters who are chauffeured have little reason to learn the geography through which they are driven. If they travel by transit, they soon learn the rudimentary layout of the city, or get lost. They also learn to read maps as a sort of self-defense against getting lost. Today's young drivers, not knowing much about the metropolitan area's geography, have a great reluctance to leave their community. Only rarely do they stray from their community and then mainly along the major highways. Finally, when they become adults and still have not learned to read maps they may have a higher propensity for getting lost on unfamiliar roads. In any case, the confused driver, unfamiliar with his surroundings, is becoming an ever-increasing driving hazard, particularly on the high-speed freeways where one driver, creeping along to read a sign or to find an exit, can

3. Arnold Gesell and Frances L. Ilg, *The Child from Five to Ten*, Harper & Row, New York, 1946, page 443; Arnold Gesell, Frances L. Ilg, Louise Bates Ames, *Youth: The Years from Ten to Sixteen*, Harper & Row, New York, 1956, pages 496–7. Cited by permission of Harper & Row Publishers, Inc.

easily cause a chain accident. Most gas station attendants who work near freeway exits can tell tales of the confused motorist who asks, 'Am I in town X ?,' naming a locale 20, 30 and even 50 miles away. Officials feel that the problem has become so bad that some highway planners in the U.S.[4] have seriously proposed electronic route-guidance systems, with road-side sensors and special displays inside the car to help motorists find their destinations. So far no system has gotten past the conceptual state, since road maps are still cheaper.

Besides the young, there are also the poor and the aged who fail to make many trips they ought to make. In the case of the poor, much has been said and written of their problems in getting to and from work. Many solutions have been proposed including special bus routes from urban ghettos to suburban job centers, but as a whole these solutions have been very ineffective. The reason is simple. The journey to work is not the greatest transportation problem of the poor. If a person has a job, especially a full-time 7 to 4 or 8 to 5 job Monday through Friday, there is usually a way in which non-car owners can find someone to take them to work. But many employed poor do not work these hours. More likely they work in the service industries, as dishwashers or janitors, with odd hours and frequently split shifts. For these hours it is much harder to find a ride. But even these trips are not the poor's greatest concern. The unskilled jobs by their very nature tend to be temporary, last-hired-first-fired type jobs. The poor thus must frequently hunt new jobs, and in job-hunting a car is far more necessary than in holding a job. With no car for job-hunting, even in days of high employment, the poor may lack precisely the one tool – transportation – they require to pull themselves up by their own bootstraps. There are traditionally the jokes and the sneering against the poor who ask for welfare and food assistance, but still own a car. At first glance this may strike one as a misplaced sense of value; but the poor, especially the ones hopefully temporarily out of luck, rightly recognize the need for a car, for other-wise they will never be able to enter or reenter the affluent society. Many jobs in sales and services make car ownership a condition of employment and frequently require the ownership of a late-model car. The various studies which have suggested giving the poor cars as the

4. 'Route Guidance', Five Reports, Highway Research Record No. 265, Highway Research Board, Washington, D.C., 1968.

cheapest solution to their transportation problems may have made the suggestion tongue in cheek, but certainly had the only true solution.

Still the plight of the young and the middle-aged poor is nothing compared to the plight of the aged. The aged have never traveled much, and in past societies there was little need for them to move around. The world they needed was with them or came to them. Not so in our modern society. Today, the aged have an ever-increasing need for local trip-making and, as society becomes more automobile-dependent, less opportunity to do so.

With the increased ease of food preparation and the near universality of thermostat-controlled furnaces, increasing numbers of the aged maintain their own households. In the U.S. in 1972, 28 per cent of those over 65 years of age lived alone in one-person households. This presents a sharp increase from the 19 per cent ten years earlier. What drives the aged finally to move to old-age homes or to their children's home is frequently their inability to perform the local trip-making that is required to maintain a household. There is the need to shop for food. Here the aged are handicapped not only by their inability to drive, but also by their restricted physical strength. Once there were the milkmen, the breadmen, the icemen, the vegetable men who peddled their wares door to door. Then there were the grocery stores who made regular deliveries. Today, the routemen have nearly vanished and grocers that deliver are few. Where they do exist they charge considerably higher prices than the supermarkets. This means many aged who live alone shop by taxi. The boy at the supermarket loads the bags into the cab, and the cabbie for a tip carries them into the house.

The aged, when they are sick, need health care and the attention of a doctor, but, because of the hassle and cost associated with getting to a doctor's office, may frequently not receive the attention they need. While public-health nurses will make regular home visits, the physician's house-call has disappeared with the routeman. Doctors feel that they can give better health care in their office and the hospital emergency room, where they are surrounded by all the required hardware for diagnosis and treatment, than in the home, where they can rely only on their little black bag. Thus, the aged must rely on relatives and friends to chauffeur them, and when these don't exist, or are not to be inconvenienced, on taxis. The taxi has become increasingly the transportation system of the aged and the poor. According to the Northern Middlesex Area study, the aged are more likely to make their trips by taxi than any other age group and the median family income of taxi passengers is significantly lower than that of travelers by any other mode, including the public bus.

We have described the lack of trip-making in the auto-dependent society. This appears to contradict the observable fact that there is a steady rise in trip-making. All over the world auto trips are increasing faster than the population, faster than the reduced ridership in public transportation and probably faster than automobile ownership. Each year the statistical average person takes more trips and travels further. Since even in North America these trends show no abating, one should expect over time that the automobile will supply all the socially needed trips.

While on a per capita basis trip-making is increasing, it is highly doubtful that purposeful trip-making is. The new trips made this year, but not last year, are generally trips to overcome deficiencies in transportation that the automobile represents. Travel in an urban area is the transporting that is needed to sustain the activity and land-use patterns of the urban area. If residence and workplace are co-located, as was usual prior to the industrial revolution, trips between residence and work are not necessary. If they are separated, as in the tracked city, and more and more randomly arranged, as in the rubber city, not only trips but ever longer trips to and from work become the *modus vivendi*. Though the activity and land-use patterns determine the need for travel, and the availability of transportation these patterns, this accounts only in part for the required trip-making.

Urban trips can be divided into three broad classes: intrinsic trips, extrinsic trips and transport-generated trips. Intrinsic trips are those which have no real destination, and where the traveler makes the trip as an end in itself. Into this group fall recreational walking, running and the 'Sunday drive', be it by surrey, sleigh or automobile. All joy-riding and racing trips, regardless of the mode, belong to this group.

An extrinsic trip is the conventional one, where some goods or people are moved from one place to another. It is valued as a means to an end. The trip to and from work, the general business trip, the shopping trip, all belong to this group. Also in this group belong social and recreational travel, where the object is to go somewhere, not travel itself, that is the trip to visit friends, to attend a football game, to go to a restaurant, the theater or cinema.

The third group of trips are the transport-generated trips. These are the trips that are needed to support the transport system, to make it function. Historically, the oldest trip of this kind was the travel necessary

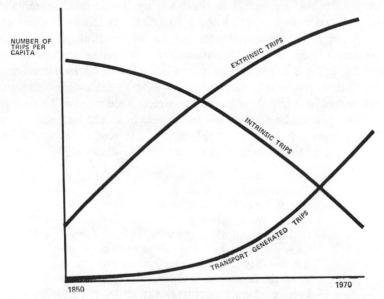

Fig. 3. *Relative change in urban travel by types of trips*

to take a horse to the smithy to have it shoed. Today, there are the auto trips to the service station and garage for fuel, repair and parts. To this must be added the dead hauling of the empty bus or truck to pick up a load, or, in the parlance of bus operators, the non-revenue mileage. Travel in search of a parking place is in the same group. These trips make up a considerable amount of the traffic in highly congested areas. Finally, but by no means least – quite to the contrary – there are all the trips auto-drivers generate for the sole purpose of serving auto passengers – to pick someone up, to drop someone off. The driver's trips to chauffeur the young and the elderly belong in this group, as well as special trips by drivers to pick up and discharge car-pool passengers.

While in these cases the drivers' travel is 'transport-generated', the trips of the passengers are 'extrinsic' trips.

Over time the distribution of these three trip types has not remained constant, nor have they all increased (see Figure 3). Intrinsic trip-making has declined. Sunday afternoon is, at least in the United States, no longer the time when the greatest number of cars are on the road. Sunday driving, or generally intrinsic driving, has declined sharply for the past two or three decades. And if recreational driving is today on the decline, the recreational walk has for all practical purposes disappeared. There is today a renaissance in bicycling and maybe in walking, but it is nowhere as prevalent as it used to be. In the walking city, with its poor transportation, space was at a premium. People lived and worked in cramped quarters. The streets were narrow. To escape, to have a place to breathe, people had to get out and go for a walk. The German poet Goethe (1749–1832) conveys this need for escape in his play *Faust*, where the hero describes an Easter Sunday walk.

> Turn about from these heights
> To look towards the city.
> Out of the hollow, dark gate
> Bursts a motley throng.
> Each happily absorbs the sun.
> They celebrate the Lord's Resurrection,
> Because they themselves are resurrected
> From the damp rooms of low-ceiling houses,
> From the bondages of work and trade,
> From the pressure of gables and roofs,
> From the streets' pressing confinement,
> From the churches' reverend night
> Have they all been brought to the light.

Today, with more space in which to carry on our activities, with roomier houses, apartments, stores and workplaces, with wider streets, with a cleaner urban environment through better sewage, smokeless fuel, the disappearance of insect-attracting horse and cow dung, the need to escape through purely intrinsic travel is no longer as important as it once must have been.

Extrinsic trip-making began to grow with the larger plants and the production specialization of the industrial revolution, the truck and the automobile. Finally, a further growth in extrinsic trips occurred when the use of private cars for the hauling of goods, particularly shopping, replaced the delivery services and the door-to-door salesman. Though all these factors have contributed to the steady increase in the number and length of extrinsic trips, this by no means explains the entire growth of urban movements in the post-war decades.

Far greater than the growth of extrinsic trips has been the expansion of the transport-generated trips. Today, in the United States, these account for most of the growth in urban movements over and above what is due to the rise in the urban population. A decade ago, transportation surveys already showed that more than a fifth of all automobile trips were generated to serve the passengers, and there is every indication that these trips are increasing. About half involve dead hauling the car, and point up the waste motion generated by the automobile.

There are no direct measures of the growth in the transportation-generated trips. From our own analysis of a number of U.S. metropolitan transportation surveys, we estimate that by the late 1960s these accounted for a fourth of all auto driver trips and had grown at an annual rate of 10 per cent since the mid-1950s. This is about three times the growth rate of all trip generation. On the average, the transportation-generated trips involve shorter distances than the work trips; thus they account for less of the vehicle miles than they do of the trip generation.

Whatever the precise growth figure may be, it is certainly a startling growth and a growth which should give concern. Every year, people generate more auto trips just to place the private car into a position where it can be serviced, or where it can pick up someone who needs a ride, or to haul it home after it was serviced or has discharged its passengers. In the growing concern with air pollution, it is well to note that every year a greater proportion of this pollution is not generated by the auto that is needed to transport something, but by the auto that is driven through the urban scene so that it can be in a position to transport something. Every commercial transport system will do its best – in the name of efficiency – to minimize its non-revenue mileage. Meanwhile our all-efficient modern society is turning to a land-use pattern and a transportation system that requires a disproportionately larger number of trips not to transport something, or someone, but to chauffeur empty cars. The modern suburban housewife is the prime victim of this polluting inefficiency, for she makes many of these trips. The chauffeuring mother is today so truly a symbol of the affluent society that the Ford Motor Company could run a television ad in the late sixties in which a young bride proclaimed: 'I promise to love, honor, obey and spend half my life in a station wagon.' With the twentieth-century technological revolution in the kitchen and in transportation, the modern mother has been freed from the stove to be chained to the wheel.

In former times, the great number of intrinsic trips were a pathological sign of the mobility crisis that haunted cities. Because of inadequate and cumbersome transportation, residences, activity centers and work spaces had to have direct access to one another and be squeezed into the narrowest possible confines. The result was that activities overlapped with each other, that people were continually confronted by one another and constantly got on each other's nerves. In short, it was a sign of the city where there was no real privacy.

Today the mounting transportation-generated trips are a pathological sign of the mobility crisis that haunts metropolitan areas. Because of total reliance on flexible automobile transportation, residences, activity centers and workplaces have no direct access to one another and are spread over vast areas of land. The result is that access between activities is limited to formal trip-making, and the people in different activities have little chance of encountering one another. In short, it is a sign of a metropolitan area where there is no real community.

There is a lack of community in the auto-centered society because large groups of the population lack the mobility which is demanded for full participation in this society. Better transportation can probably not solve this problem. No transport system that one can imagine can overcome the alienation of modern society and again bind it into a communal whole. Just for argument's sake, assume science had created the magic carpet, free as manna from heaven. The carpet glides through the air, at 60 or 100 mph, covered by an air-conditioned cupola. It does not pollute. It can enter buildings through doors and windows. If not in use, it can be rolled up and stuck into a corner. The operation of this vehicle is so simple and safe that anyone can operate it who is capable of walking alone to the end of the block. This science-fiction marvel, since it is free, available to all but the housebound, can fulfil any trip-making needs that a society can have. No one can say: 'I didn't make it because I had no way to go.' Different alibis would be needed. If people want to be somewhere, they can be there. Still, even this system would not solve the basic social problems. With massive auto transportation, people have found a way to isolate themselves; a way to avoid confrontation; a way to privacy among their peer group. With help of the auto, they have stratified the urban landscape like a checker board, here a piece for the young married, there one for health care, here one for shopping, there one for the swinging jet set, here one for industry, there one for the aged, here one for the rich in their fifties, there a ghetto for the *Untermensch* – be they poor or racially despised. When people move from square to square, they move purposefully, determinedly (not cruising for the sake of cruising). They see nothing except what they are determined to see. Everything else is shut out from their experience. People prefer to travel on limited-access roads rather than arterials and side streets, because on limited-access roads they are not confronted by oncoming traffic, by children darting about, by cross-traffic. Here everyone travels in the same direction at more or less the same speed. In fact, they wish that others would be even more like themselves, for in traffic people cuss with equal vehemence the cars that pass them as those that block their pathway. People like to insist on air-conditioned cars to keep the weather and the traffic noises at arm's length. In driving about they only rarely see the surrounding sights, not only as drivers, but as passengers as well. The fact that auto-transported children are easily lost in their own communities and often do not know their city's most rudimentary arterial road network shows how much one can travel without paying attention to the surroundings.

In the short run, this behavior makes a lot of sense. Privacy is guaranteed. No one is forced to deal with extraneous events. People can go about their business purposefully and efficiently. While people may live for the moment, they exist over time. This privatization which society practices so joyously and relentlessly through the use of auto-mobiles, and which could not be practiced if there were no cars, is easily the bane of the individual's existence over time. By reducing most activities to those that are purposeful and efficient, a person sacrifices the antennae that recognize change and that can warn of impending dangers. The alienation that abounds everywhere, the increased feeling that people are no longer masters of their fate, that they are picked on and put upon, that they are buoyed by forces they do not control, and that those in control do not understand their needs, hopes and desires, all this may well be due to the fact that too many, from head of state to social outcast, are too much and too unrelentingly pursuing the business of the moment too privately, too purposefully, too efficiently. Any system that in this environment gives society even more auto-like transportation, even more private insulated transportation, to skip from one purposive activity to the next, be it a business deal, a school examination or a sexual orgy, can over time make today's alienation only worse tomorrow.

While unequally distributed mobility is the readily apparent social crisis of the automobile-centered society, the basic problem is not that the young and the aged and the poor have not enough mobility, but rather that the rest have too much mobility. The transportation crisis of the modern society is thus a crisis of overabundance. Society has turned from yesterday's overcrowded cities in horror, to the space-generating automobile and all the privacy it can bestow. But as the old saying goes, 'a rolling stone gathers no moss'. Thus, today, the affluent, the fully mobile ones, run from one activity to another like wound-up automatons, in the search for privacy, non-confrontation and peace, all qualities which they shall never find until they realize that one cannot run away from life's problems but must face them, until there is a realization that people need not just transportation, but collocation as well – forced, peaceful togetherness, where one can work out life's little problems and misunderstandings, where one can contemplate and observe, where one can be both passive observer and active partici-pant, where the world is where one is, not here and yonder. Trans-portation cannot be the only way in which people come together, it is too complicated, too purposive, too planned. A city, a society, any co-operative enterprise, is both collocation and transportation. If it is either at the expense of the other it is the stinking mess the walking city was, or the organized chaos of alienation today's sprawling metro-polis is or threatens to become.

CHAPTER 8

The Economic Crisis

The economic crisis in urban transportation has its roots in the policy that the cost of transportation, like those of other market products, should be borne by the user. In this chapter we show that most of the benefits of urban transportation accrue not to the traveler, but to third parties such as real-estate developers, retailers and employers whose land or services have become accessible through the existence of transportation. Furthermore, we contend that urban transportation cannot exist solely on fare-box income but must be subsidized, if it is to influence the location of residences, commerce, industry and public institutions. To explain these somewhat intricate relationships, we use the arguments of economic theory. The reader who is not interested in such theoretical discussions may prefer to proceed directly to Chapter 9.

Economic theory holds that in capitalist societies the 'market' is the major force that allocates resources to transportation. Even though there are policy decisions and other public 'interferences' with the market, all these activities are built around the assumption that the market is the principal determinant of transportation prices and outputs. What economic theory means by 'market' and 'market behavior' can be seen from the simplified, yet accurate, model of the relationship between supply and demand, which is shown in Figures 4–6.

Figure 4 represents a demand relationship. Let us assume it represents the total demand for automobiles of a certain quality. The vertical axis contains the different prices for which the automobile could sell and the horizontal axis presents the quantities of the automobile that consumers would be willing to buy at various prices. For example, the demand relationship shown in Figure 4 assumes that, at a price of $2,000 per automobile, consumers would purchase 100,000 automobiles. At a price of $1,000 per car, the market demand would increase to 300,000 cars. An important assumption implicit in the demand relationship is that the lower the price of the good or service in question, the

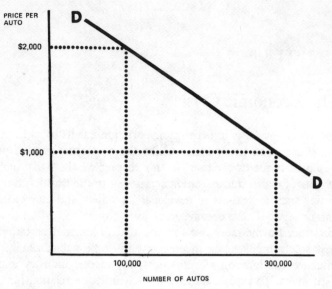

Fig. 4. *Demand for autos*

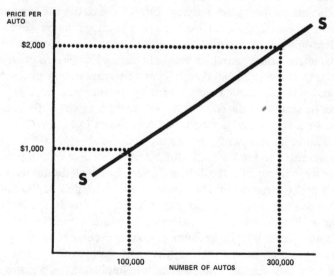

Fig. 5. *Supply of autos*

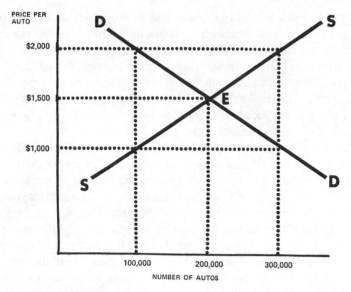

Fig. 6. *Market for autos*

more of it people will be willing to purchase, provided other factors influencing the purchase decision remain unchanged. In the case of the automobile, for example, if the price were cut in half, people who had decided not to purchase automobiles because of income, taste or the availability of substitute travel modes would now find the automobile an attractive alternative. Similarly, some families or individuals who decided to purchase only one automobile might decide to purchase two. The point is simply that more will be demanded at lower prices.

If there are buyers to demand goods and services, there must also be sellers to supply goods and services for a market to occur. Figure 5 portrays a supply relationship which is the opposite of the demand relationship. At higher prices, where buyers will buy less, sellers are willing to supply more. To make the example symmetrical, we assume that at a price of $2,000 per automobile sellers are willing to supply 300,000 automobiles, and at a price of $1,000 they are only willing to supply 100,000. The crucial assumption in this supply relationship is that prices must rise to induce sellers to supply larger quantities of a good or service to the market, or that, in a competitive market, sellers will at any price bring to the market all of the goods or services they can sell at a profit. A competitive market by definition means there are many buyers and sellers, with ease of entry and exit to the market, and that no individual buyer or seller is large enough to influence the market. Thus, each seller will be able to sell all he can supply at the going price. The reason the seller does not supply more is that the cost of producing the additional supply would be more than the revenue brought in from the market at the prevailing price.

Put differently, the supply relationship assumes that production occurs under conditions of *diminishing returns*. This means the cost of producing additional output with a given size plant is higher than the production of the preceding output. If the cost for the additional output were less than or equal to the cost of the preceding output, then the competitive seller would have produced more and brought it to market at the going price. The reasons for diminishing returns relate to conditions of production. For example, after a certain point the capacity of a plant is so burdened that additional output generates bottlenecks and breakdowns at different points in the production process. Or the additional demand for productive factors (labor, raw materials, etc.) will begin to push up the cost of these inputs and hence the cost of production.

In Figure 6 the supply and demand relationships shown in Figures 4 and 5 are placed on a single chart. This figure shows the market outcome where buyers and sellers behave in the manner assumed in the previous two figures. In Figure 6, an equilibrium market between buyers and sellers is established at point E. At point E sellers are willing to supply 200,000 automobiles at a price of $1,500. Buyers are willing to buy that number of automobiles at that price and the market is cleared. There are neither shortages nor excess inventories. To see why the market, left to its own devices, would reach this equilibrium let us assume that sellers first come to market with 300,000 autos at a price of $2,000. Given the behavior of the buyers, only 100,000 autos would be sold. In other words, if the price was above the equilibrium, the pressures of the market would begin to force it down. If, on the other hand, the price was initially below the market price at, say, $1,000, the pressures of the market would force the price upwards. At a price of $1,000 buyers would be willing to buy 300,000 autos. But sellers would bring only 100,000 to market. As a result, a shortage would exist at that price. Buyers now would begin to offer higher prices for the available supply. The increase in price in the market would induce sellers to bring more autos on the market. It is only at a price of $1,500 that buyers and sellers achieve equilibrium and there would be no tendency for further movement in either quantity or price.

The example helps to explain why the concept of the market as an instrument of social decision-making has been attractive to many social theoreticians over the years. The decisions about the quantity, quality and price of the commodities which a society uses are arrived at through the interaction of buyers and sellers. The decision of the market is a reflection of the choices of those who participate in the market, not the coercion of state power. In a world that operates along the lines of our simplified auto market, one is hard-pressed to advocate changes for the general good. However, the world acts only approximately like our example. The factors that do not permit the world to act as the model cause the market model to give off signals which, if not entirely incorrect, are inaccurate enough to cause problems to the urban society.
• In fact, these factors are so deeply intertwined in the larger social order that the market has become a totally inadequate instrument for alleviating urban transport problems.

Simple market analysis of transportation runs as follows: In a market economy, sellers can sell only that which buyers seek to possess in the absence of any outside coercion. Assuming existing residential and employment patterns, consumers of urban transportation services have a choice between public transport and private automobile transport. Over the past three decades consumers have continually abandoned public transport in favor of the auto. In face of such an overwhelming choice, the policy issue for economists and planners is thus to devise methods of making the marketplace choice more meaningful by making auto transport more efficient. The naïve version of this view holds that policy should be totally automobile-oriented. A more sophisticated view recognizes that some public transit is needed for purposes of 'balance' if automobile-based metropolitan areas are to remain operational. In either case we are not given any ground for a significant break with the automobile-based post-Second World War transportation policy which has caused highway concrete to spread from the United States to market-oriented economies around the world.[1]

For those who oppose coercive forms of decision-making, the above view becomes positively immobilizing. Who are we to impose our particular tastes and preferences upon a society which freely and uncoercively arrived at the decision to expand metropolitan areas around the automobile?

On the other hand, if our observations about the damage done by the automobile to the urban form are correct, what should be done? It is our belief that this simplistic market view is only partly correct and that a more complete understanding of the urban transportation market demonstrates that significant alterations in transport policy are consistent with the need to allow consumers noncoercive choices. Simply put, we believe that those who attempt to rationalize the present transportation predicament as being in some sense the 'will of the people', as expressed through the market, malign the people *and* the market.

The principal problem with this simplistic approach is that it does not consider that the 'externalities' of transportation outweigh the benefits to the traveler. In the economist's parlance, 'externalities' refer to those effects that result from a market transaction which are not accounted for in the costs and benefits calculated in the marketplace. For example, a manufacturer moves into a town and causes the railroad to build a spur into that town to accommodate the business the manufacturer generates. This creates an 'external economy' for others in the town who can now avail themselves of the newly instituted rail service. The manufacturer can't charge the new users for the benefit which it

1. While a significant increase in automobile usage in urban areas in Eastern Europe has occurred in recent years, despite the existence of good to excellent public transport, this by no means demonstrates that even East European consumers prefer the auto to public transport in urban areas. The increased auto consumption of these non-market-oriented economies has nothing to do with the work trip or other routine urban travel. Rather, the increased private transport consumption is a result of higher standards of living and the desire to have access to places such as the countryside which can't be reached by public transport, as was the case with early auto usage in the capitalist countries. To the extent that good public transport permits this pattern to continue into the future, the impact of increased auto usage in Eastern Europe will be far different from that observed in capitalist countries.

created for them, and consequently economists say that the manufacturer created an external benefit or economy. On the other hand, a firm whose smoke stack pollutes the air with sulfur fumes creates external diseconomies or external costs for the local householders who have to repaint their homes more frequently. In the absence of some type of payment to these householders, the firm is able to shift part of the cost of its product from its customers to a third party, the householders.

Externalities in transportation exist whenever a trip is made to engage in some activity at the destination. In the last chapter we saw that intrinsic or 'end in itself' travel which generates no externalities was far less important than extrinsic or 'means to an end' travel which generates externalities. Furthermore, the 'transport-generated trips', that is the trips needed to maintain the transport system, are on the rise and these too generate externalities. Thus, for the transport consumer travel is generally only a means to an end, and from the point of view of the traveler the less travel involved in carrying out an activity the better. For most other goods and services the degree of intrinsic satisfaction increases with consumption – the consumption of food, clothing, shelter, recreation, etc., viewed as end products or as the satisfactions which the economic system is supposed to produce. Transportation, with the exception of a small portion of movement such as the Sunday drive, is generally useful only to the extent that it helps to attain satisfaction from some other sources.

Transportation also differs in a second way from other consumer goods and services. The traveler interacts at his destination with friends, retailers, employers and others; all these people act as third parties to the marketplace transaction between the traveler and the transport provider. The degree of third-party, or external, involvement in the consumption of transportation is far higher than for any other category of consumer goods. Thus, as we approach the analysis of the transportation market, we must be aware that the degree of individual satisfaction attained from travel *per se* is lower than for most other consumer outputs and that the degree of external involvement is far higher.

None would deny that, overall, the continual improvements in transportation technology had external impacts on the larger society. The impacts are both costs and benefits. Railroads were not allowed into the nineteenth-century cities precisely because they generated external costs, they polluted. One major reason for the current advocacy of public transportation in the larger metropolitan areas is the fact that public transit generates less pollution than automobile transportation, and thus presents an external benefit. Improved urban transportation in general has benefited the urban areas by permitting them to grow beyond the size of walking cities and to take full advantage of the economies of scale which the industrial revolution and modern technologies offer. The spatial, economic and social arrangements of the tracked and rubber city in contrast to the walking city are the external benefits, or costs, of improved urban transportation.

Not only urban transportation, but transportation in general creates external economies. For example, land grants were an important incentive for the development of the transcontinental railroads in the United States and Canada. Today, shipping companies that haul on consignment find that without government subsidies they cannot survive. In the 'old days', when shippers bought their goods overseas and sold them at their destination, these sales captured the external benefits of shipping and made it a profitable venture. Air travel presents a more current example of the externalities accompanying transportation service. Airline companies increasingly invest their capital in resort hotels and tourist attractions. At the same time they offer air fare discounts to those who will avail themselves of these other goods and services in the form of 'packaged tours'.

Though, under most circumstances, providers of external benefits are unable to capture a return from them, in transportation the suppliers of transport services often can. A transport supplier can generate external benefits by making formerly inaccessible real estate accessible, and can capture these benefits if he owns this real estate. This was true of the land developers of the walking cities who built bridges to make land across swamps and rivers accessible to the rest of the city. It was also true of the developers who instituted ferry services, and it is most clearly true of the streetcar developers of the tracked city era. In each case the transport innovation was not profitable in and of itself, but rather was profitable because the entrepreneur captured a gain external to the transport market.

The operation of the market usually requires that in order to remain in business the suppliers of goods or services need only receive a profit from the sale of their output. In transportation, however, frequently the profit from capturing externalities far outweighs the profit from supplying the transport service. From this relationship arises the problem that the external benefit can usually be achieved only when passenger volumes are greater than those which would be most profitable if only transportation were supplied.

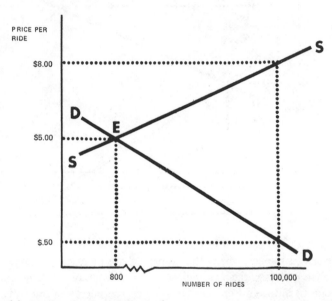

Fig. 7. (a) *Market for transport services*

This problem is illustrated in Figure 7a, which depicts the market for some particular transport service. In that market an equilibrium is achieved at a price of $5 per ride with 8,000 rides sold. But in order for this particular service to generate external benefits either to the suppliers of the transport service, to the larger society, or to both, travel volume must reach at least 100,000 rides. Given the market demand for this particular service, this volume can be attained only at a fare of 50c per ride. Given the cost of providing the service, however, the fare would have to be $8 per ride to induce the transport supplier to invest in the necessary equipment to carry 100,000 passengers. If the profits from

exploitation of an external benefit were great enough to allow an entrepreneur to subsidize the transport system and still have a larger profit
than would be possible from the provision of transport alone, then he
would undertake the subsidy. In many instances this has been the case.

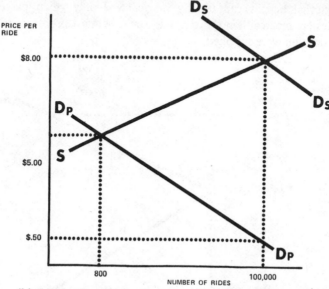

Fig 7. (b) *Market for transport services with private and social demand*

In other instances where the transport supplier cannot capture the
external benefits, the external social benefit may be real and large
enough to induce government to provide the necessary subsidy.

To clarify this idea we redraw Figure 7(a) as 7(b). The figures are
identical but for one addition. Through the point on the supply curve
represented by 100,000 rides we have drawn a second demand curve
labeled D_S. The original curve is labeled D_P, indicating that it is still
the total demand of all private users of that particular transport service.
However, since there are wider social benefits beyond those for the
individual travelers using that service, let us say that a demand curve,
D_S, represents the value to society of different volumes of travel on that
system. As can be seen, at each and every price, the social demand is
larger than the private demand. These social benefits translate into the
benefits which accrue to those owning real estate made more accessible,

those whose shops can now serve a wider market and those whose places of employment are now accessible to a larger labor market. Thus we would expect pressures for public subsidy from those who gain these benefits. If this were the case, subsidy sufficient to increase transport volume to 100,000 would occur.

The issues of externalities are often overlooked by economists in analyzing the transport market. This occurs because many analyses are limited to questions of the choice of transport mode within a pre-existing spatial context. However, as we have seen, spatial relationships themselves depend upon transport modes and relative transport availability. This is readily acknowledged by most policy makers who apply market tools to transport problems. But, the analytic tools are better suited to the more partial analyses, where either the choice of mode or the choice of spatial location are investigated, holding the other constant. The result is that studies do not investigate the ways in which urban space interacts with transport. Instead, studies of transport are discourses and policies based upon the demand and supply of various urban travel modes in a given spatial context, rather than the relationship between transportation modes and the spatial location patterns.

The narrowing of the transportation problem through assuming that spatial location patterns are given has as a consequence that the problem of transport subsidies is approached with great timidity. In the narrow context, subsidies appear to lead to a wasteful misuse of scarce resources. However, if third-party benefits are considered, subsidies may in fact not be a misuse of scarce resources, but represent an efficient allocation of resources. Economists who look at transportation in the narrow context usually try to develop policy prescriptions that eliminate or at least minimize subsidies. Most commonly they try to find 'cures' for the subsidy that can be traced to the transportation capacities that are needed to handle the rush-hour traffic.

But a vital local economy requires that urban transportation is able to handle the rush-hour work trips. To accommodate these work trips, the transport system must have the capacity to carry considerably more passengers during peak than off-peak hours. This means, however, that most of a system's capacity is idle most of the time. Since the transport industry requires considerable investment in fixed capital, the under-utilization of this capital imposes a significant cost which must be paid one way or another.

The existence of underutilized capital gives off signals which are contradictory if interpreted only in the narrow context. This situation is illustrated in Figure 8. That figure shows a hypothetical demand curve for transport service. It also has two cost curves, one illustrating the cost of providing the service, the other the cost of supplying addi-

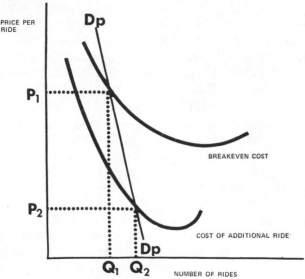

Fig. 8. *Transport costs and market demand*

tional amounts of service. The top curve represents the average total cost of providing the service. It takes into account both the operating and capital costs for the service. The bottom curve just measures the additional operating costs incurred for additional passengers. Thus, it measures the additional costs of fuel or drivers (in the case of buses) to serve the additional passengers with a given rolling stock and plant.[2]

2. This situation is referred to as one of increasing returns to scale, in contrast to the more usual case of diminishing returns to scale previously discussed. For a further discussion of this topic in relation to transportation see *Transport* (Penguin Books, Baltimore, 1968) edited by Denis Munby (especially part 2). For a more general discussion of the entire topic of peak loads and increasing returns see Turvey, ed. *Public Enterprises* (Penguin Books, Baltimore).

The market has two criteria for successful operation. The first is that total costs must not exceed total revenue for any appreciable period of time. The second is that as long as the additional amount of output is more than or equal to the additional cost of providing that output, it should be provided. According to the first criterion, the fare should be at P_1 and the volume of rides sold should be at Q_1. However, profit maximization also requires that as long as additional revenue from additional output is greater than additional cost, output should be expanded. In our example, then, output should be expanded to Q_2 and price lowered to P_2. However, at that price and output the transport provider's revenues would not cover the total cost. Thus, the need for large investments to satisfy the peak load widens the gap between the solutions offered by the two criteria of the market and consequently heightens the subsidy issue.

The problem of peak and off-peak usage of facilities is not unique to transportation. Resort hotels charge more during the season when the demand for their facilities is the greatest than during the off-season. Theaters charge different rates for Saturday evenings than Wednesday matinees, reflecting the variation in demand for tickets. Restaurants which charge high prices in the evening often serve inexpensive 'businessmen's lunches' during the day. Telephone rates also vary with the time of day, reflecting the differences in demand.

The idea of charging different rates for the same good or service depending upon when the buyer wishes to obtain the output is consistent with the operation of a competitive market. Since the room capacity of the hotel, the seating and cooking capacity of the restaurant, the seating capacity of the theater and the line capacity of the telephone company are designed to serve the peak demand for these outputs, it is the peak-time user of these outputs who pays the additional cost of this additional capacity. The off-peak user, on the other hand, contributes little or nothing to the capacity-creating cost. From the standpoint of the seller, the idea of charging the off-peak user less is just plain good business sense. Fixed capital stock generates costs regardless of the quantity of the output. If the lower charges induce increased use of fixed capital in off periods at least loss is being minimized.

In the area of urban transportation there are many examples of capacity created for peak purposes: there is the lane capacity of urban expressways, the passenger-carrying capacity of subways and buses, the passenger capacity of commuter railroads and even the size of the taxi fleet. All of these examples have one thing in common: the creation of sufficient transport capacity to carry the rush-hour passenger around the metropolitan area. However, unlike the other industries faced with problems of peak loads, the pricing mechanism in the area of urban transportation operates in what, by the standard of the narrower economic approach to transit, is usually regarded as a perverse manner. It is the peak-period railroad commuter who receives a lower fare. Bridge and tunnel authorities around the United States sell books or passes which give the regular user of these facilities, the peak-period commuter, a reduced toll. Even when the peak-period motorist is not given special discounts, neither is the motorist charged more than off-peak users. There is no charge at all on most 'freeways'. Subways and buses, too, charge a single fare. This may vary with distance but rarely, if ever, does it vary with the time of use. This situation arises partly from the difficulty of imposing differential charges on urban transport users. More importantly, the situation reflects the role of transport in creating urban external economies. The economists' standard jaundiced view of transport subsidy and peak subsidy in particular comes from analyzing transport as essentially a service whose major beneficiary is the direct user. However, if the external economies are seen as the dominant outcome peak-load subsidy makes sense. The movement of the work force at the beginning and end of the workday is one of the most vital contributions of transport to supporting the spatial arrangements of the metropolitan economy. Thus subsidy to the peak user becomes an important factor in permitting the operation of that economy, and the removal of the subsidy with its attendant reduction in travel must be evaluated within the broader spatial location patterns rather than within the narrow one of direct user benefits. However, all this does not imply that peak-period pricing should not be used to channel travelers from one mode to another; for instance by placing high tolls on auto access to induce commuters to use public modes.

To the extent then that subsidy is a fact of life for urban transportation, the questions which we must look at are: how much subsidy, who should provide it and to which modes? The answers must be cast in terms of their effect on urban space. While it is general knowledge that public transport modes receive some form of subsidy, the extent of subsidy to the auto is less well-known. Indeed one rather popular view in the United States is that auto users pay the full cost of auto facilities. It is argued that the construction and maintenance cost of highways are completely paid from sales and excise taxes on motor fuels, oils, tires and vehicles as well as tolls. In the United States many mechanisms exist which insure that the revenues from these sources are used for automobile- and highway-related public expenditures. In fact about 98 per cent of construction, maintenance and police costs for the primary highways does come from these sources. This does not mean, however, that the auto is not subsidized in other ways.

The highway trust funds in the United States insure that tax revenues from motor vehicles and related products are used for auto transport purposes. All revenues from motor vehicle sources are placed in such funds and then disbursed according to a set of guidelines which limit their use to highway-related activity. Such trust funds exist at the federal level and in most states. Even without discussing the highway-related expenditures not paid from these funds, the very existence of these funds is subsidy. Previously it was noted that the trust funds were established only after it became clear that tax revenues from highway uses were beginning to exceed expenditures on highway activity. Thus, the funds were only established after auto-related expenses no longer required financing from general tax revenues.

Governments levy all sorts of taxes on all sorts of things. These taxes range from taxes on income and profits, to taxes on transactions (sales taxes) to taxes on specific products (such as tobacco and alcohol) to taxes on real estate to taxes on meals, and so forth. The point is that a principal reason for these taxes is the generation of revenue to support various projects and programs which governments undertake. As with most other things, government support is a scarce resource which must be allocated among seemingly infinite needs. To set up a special fund, in which a certain portion of government revenue is placed and spent without regard to other projects and programs on an indefinite basis and without regard to changing conditions and needs, is in fact implicitly to subsidize that particular project or program at the expense of others which also require public funding. The fact that these funds subsidize not transport in general but only one particular mode merely accentuates the distortion. The question should be whether we need more transportation and if so what mix of modes will best serve the population, rather than where the next highway should be located. The fact that very little support is available to meet the public transport needs of society while a veritable horn of plenty exists for highways is cause for much concern. In the final analysis there is no more reason for taxes on automobiles and related products to be devoted to highway-related activities than for the proceeds of the tax on restaurant meals to be devoted to the construction and maintenance of restaurants! User-related taxes, collected under the previously described schemes, do not relate the charges to the time or place at which automobiles are used. Thus, off-peak users are paying the same amount as peak users for capacity costs generated by the peak user. This in turn implies an underpricing or subsidy to the peak user and, as a result, it acts as an incentive for excessive use of urban highways during peak periods. The indications are that the underpriced capacity is expensive capacity. In 1962 William Vickery estimated that the capital cost of providing sufficient lane capacity for all the highway traffic in Washington, D.C., during peak periods would come to $23,000 per peak-period car.[3] This means a charge of $9 per round trip, assuming 250 workdays a year and allowing a 10 per cent gross return which a comparable investment in the private sector would have to earn to cover interest, amortization and property and corporate income taxes. These costs are over and above the costs for highway maintenance and parking. Clearly if user charges in line with these costs were imposed upon urban automobile commuters, either spatial relationships in metropolitan areas would be far different or more public transport would be used or some combination of the two would occur. It would definitely mean a significant upgrading in quality of public transport service.

The subsidy is even greater than merely one from the *off-peak* highway user to the *peak* highway user. The system of taxes also insures that those using *local streets* subsidize the *highway* user as they too pay the taxes which comprise the highway funds. Local streets and arterials receive little, if any, support from the highway funds. They are sup-

3. William Vickery, 'Pricing in Urban and Suburban Transport', *American Economic Review, Papers and Proceedings*, May 1963, pages 452–65.

ported from locally raised revenues. Defenders of the system of highway finance are quick to argue that since local streets and roads serve the function of access to local property, they should quite properly be paid from local sources. This particular argument has its greatest validity on the most underutilized rural backroads. However, it quickly loses validity as we begin to approach the denser sectors of any metropolitan area. Indeed, one would be quite hard pressed in attempting to argue that the traffic clogging almost any crosstown street of Manhattan is on that street to reach a particular piece of property on the street. There is scarcely a rush-hour driver alive who does not have a favorite weave of back streets to get from home to work on any day and under any condition. Furthermore it is absurd to try and treat different parts of the transportation system as if they were in some sense different from one another. If all the exits on urban highways ended in unpaved dirt roads full of ruts and holes, automobiles would not be as integral a part of the urban scene as they are today. Blood vessels in the human body without capillaries make as much sense as major highways without the system of local streets and roads. Good inner city streets, then, act as further incentive to the use of the automobile. In the United States and many other countries the major revenue support for these streets are the local real-estate taxes, perhaps the most regressive taxes for financing anything. The burden of the tax that finances city streets falls most heavily upon the lowest income segments of the metropolitan community. This burden is made worse by the income segregation patterns of metropolitan areas. The lower-income groups live at and around the dense core areas and the more affluent automobile commuters tend to reside in the less dense outlying areas. Since the automobile traffic from these areas passes through the lower-income communities on its way to the core areas, the costs of road maintenance and police traffic control in these communities will be higher than in the more outlying communities. In places where the metropolitan area is broken into many small cities and towns, the cost will most directly be borne by those communities around the core with the lower-income populations.

There are many other forms of subsidy which the automobile commuters in metropolitan areas receive. We will mention only the most obvious. The oil depletion allowance which the U.S. government grants amounts to a windfall for oil companies and is in effect a subsidization of gasoline costs. Oil companies are quick to point out that if the allowance is removed gasoline prices will rise. Automobile insurance rates are lower for those residing in low-density rather than high-density communities. Rates are established this way even though there is no evidence that drivers living in high-density areas are less safe drivers than those living in the low-density areas. The basis for the rate differentials is that the high-density resident is more frequently involved in accidents than the driver residing in low-density areas. Most of the congested driving takes place in high-density areas. As a result of the congestion, contributed to in no small part by the auto commuter from the low-density areas, the probability of an accident in the high-density areas is increased. Since drivers living in the high-density areas are in this environment most of the time, it is natural that their accident rate will be higher. If broader geographic definitions were used in establishing insurance rates, the cost which the suburban driver is placing upon the inner-core driver would be more equally borne. Since auto insurance is one of the largest annual costs of automobile operation, this subsidy plays an important role in inducing automobile commutation from low-density communities.

All these subsidies are positive incentives to urban sprawl and favor the residents of low-density communities who commute over long distances above the residents in high-density areas near employment centers. The depletion allowance reduces gasoline prices and with it the operating cost of automobiles. Compared to public transit modes, the out-of-pocket costs of using an automobile for any particular trip are slight indeed. The use of real-estate taxes for the maintenance of urban streets generates a subsidy from the residents of the denser communities around employment centers, who have usually lower per capita auto ownership, to the residents of low-density communities with few employment opportunities, who usually have higher per capita auto ownership. The uniform charges to peak and off-peak users and the insurance rate policies generate an internal subsidy from auto drivers residing in high-density urban areas to auto drivers residing in low-density suburban and semi-rural areas. All these subsidies make it far harder to persuade automobile owners to use public transport and to live in high-density areas where public transit can most effectively be maintained.

The auto owners' incentives to live in low-density areas in turn lead retailers, employers and other services to choose locations that are accessible by auto. The retailers have a special reason for this move. While they must furnish their clientele with free parking, they can recover some, if not all, of these costs because customers with cars will carry most of their major purchases, while those who must rely on public transit will require the delivery of these goods. Thus the subsidization of the auto owners, and particularly the auto owners in low-density areas, becomes a reinforcing pattern for continually extending the region of urban sprawl.

A further reinforcement of urban sprawl is due to land prices. Traditionally land prices at the urban fringe are lower than those near or at the core. Qualitative differences account for little of this difference in the price of land. The major variation is due to the location or closeness to those activities or phenomena which society deems either desirable or undesirable. For example, a residential location next to a noisy, dirty railroad yard is not as desirable as one on a quiet tree-lined street. It is preferable to live within walking distance of a subway, if one lives and works in an urban environment, than at a location which requires a bus trip to the subway station. It is the collective social judgement that determines the relative desirability of various locations. Land value is thus more dependent on society's actions than the actions of the individual owner. This has led numerous observers, at least since the time of Henry George at the turn of the century, to advocate that the entire increase in the value of land due to these societal actions be taxed away by society. (This would not include the improvements made to the property by placing buildings and other capital expenditures upon the land itself.) Since society and not the individual created the increase in land value, society and not the individual should be entitled to the value increment. This particular insight is one of the few on which economists all along the political spectrum find much to agree. Since the increment in land values is a reflection of social priorities, it is possible to capture this increase in a tangible form through the ownership of land. The increase in land value can to some extent be considered a measure of the social gain which is maximized through the subsidized transport system of Figure 7(b). Consequently by looking at the impact of transport changes upon the metropolitan land market we can infer much about the creation of external economies and diseconomies.

In cities where the central business district represents the center of all economic and much of the social activity of the metropolitan area, the value of land at or near the center tends to be higher than at the fringes. The relationship is shown in Figure 9 by straight lines, the so-called 'rent-bid curves'. The further the distance from the center o_f

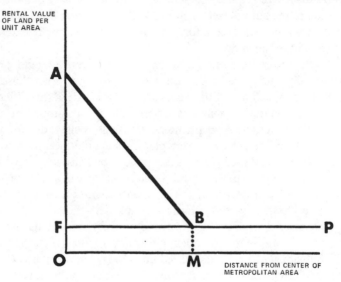

Fig. 9. *A rent-bid curve*

the city, the lower is the value of the land. The term 'rent-bid' comes from the practice of measuring the value of land by the price which its service can command, the rent. The selling price of land is nothing more than the capitalized rental value of the land. The horizontal axis in Figure 9 measures the distance in miles from the center of the metropolitan area. The vertical axis measures the rental value per unit area for land at various distances from the center. The value of land falls moving further and further from the center until it levels off, represented by line FP. FP is the value of land as farm acreage. At some point, in this case OM distance from the metropolitan center, the land loses its value as part of the metropolitan region. It then has value in terms of its agricultural income-producing potential only. This example is somewhat simplified, since land can also have value, and high and growing value, outside metropolitan areas for recreational purposes. In general the point at which the value of land reverts to its agricultural value depends upon the cost and time involved in reaching the center of the region. One hour's travel time is about as much as most people

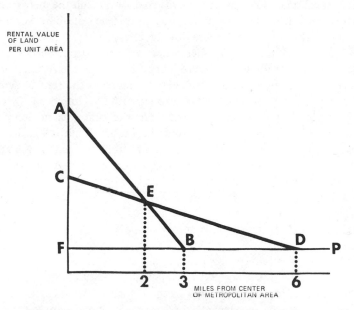

Fig. 10. *Effect of transport improvement on rent-bid curve of metropolitan area*

will commute on a daily basis. The distance covered depends upon the average speed of the mode of travel. Cost of travel, too, is an important factor. For example, it is possible to commute a considerable distance in an hour by air, but the cost is sufficient to insure that only the most affluent would even consider this alternative. Thus, in addition to speed, cost must be sufficiently low to permit a mass market if the travel mode is to affect land-use patterns significantly.

Using a graph similar to that in Figure 9 we can show the effect an improvement in transportation has upon the metropolitan land market.

Such a situation is presented in Figure 10. Line AB represents the rent-bid curve before a transportation improvement, for instance, the city before the electric streetcar. As the figure indicates, the maximum feasible distance that could be traveled in conducting daily affairs in the older metropolitan era of horsecars was about three miles. The introduction of the trolley permitted people to travel longer distances in the same travel time and at about the same cost. As a result the metropolitan area increased, in this case to an outside distance of about six miles. This new distance is represented by the line CD.

Figure 10 points out another aspect of urban transportation. In addition to extending the metropolitan area, the introduction of a transportation improvement also alters the slope of the rent-bid curve. The slope of curve CD is flatter than curve AB. This means that the price of land at different locations from the center is no longer as sensitive to the exact distance from the center. This is because the transport improvement makes land further from the center of activity more accessible to the center in terms of travel time. Land at those distances is more desirable and can command a price closer to that of land nearer the center. In addition land at the center no longer holds a monopoly position, so to speak, and its value relative to that of land at further distances falls somewhat so that the differentials are lessened.

The transport improvement in and of itself explains only part of the change in slope; the other part is explained by cost. The lower the cost of using the mode, the larger will be the market for it and consequently the greater will be the demand for land at further distances from the center. The greater the demand for land at further distances, the flatter the rent-bid curve will be. Since the transport market is a subsidized market, the slope of the curve will depend upon the extent and the method of subsidization. The greater the subsidization, the flatter the curve. If the burden of subsidy is such that it falls more heavily upon residents of the center than those of the periphery, this will flatten the curve further. Thus the distribution of the burden of the subsidies directly affects the way the transport changes alter the metropolitan land-use patterns.

The radial development which allowed the early entrepreneurs to capture a real-estate gain and hence develop land is no longer possible for operators of urban transport systems. The spatial limits of the radially structured metropolitan area have been reached for travel modes that can bring commuters into the central city in about an hour. Attempts to push development further out by public investment in highways have thus far been both ecologically and economically unsuccessful. Consequently the major concern today is to find modes which allow for more efficient movement within the built-up portion of the region. With this shift in emphasis there has also arisen a controversy around the methods of subsidizing this transport. The resolution of this controversy will have important implications for the future spatial arrangement of metropolitan areas.

One conclusion is exceedingly clear. The subsidy pattern today encourages automobile usage and discourages public transport. This in turn encourages suburbanization of the metropolitan area to the extent of completely flattening the rent-bid curve, and making the radial city model with a central core no longer applicable. This is what happened in Los Angeles, Houston and other automobile-oriented cities which had most of their growth since the Second World War. The flattening of the rent-bid curve and with it the loss of orientation around a single core reinforces the problems of isolation and lack of access which increasingly affect metropolitan areas.

With the recent resurgence of the denser communities as homes for the affluent, we are beginning to see more pressure for financing transit from public funds. The highway trust funds are becoming less the sacred cows they once were as the affluent discover the limitations of the automobile-oriented suburban communities. If we are to have healthy metropolitan areas, then good access must be available to all. However, the poor and middle class will not automatically achieve good access by the resurgence of public transport alone. Rather, they must work to achieve political power sufficient to insure that the newly created transport routes serve their needs as well as those of the rich. It is only by affecting transport policy at the political level that transport resources, allocated either through the market or by some planning body, will be turned to the task of providing good access to all. The market is similar to a computer. A computer gives back its processed data within the limitations of the program into which the data is fed. Similarly the prices and output of the transport market will only be as good as the broad policy context in which the decisions are made. At present, transport policy is such that the 'program' gives us automobile suburbs. In the future it may give better downtown mass transit for some. However, if it is to give us all better access a new transport 'program' must be fed into the political decision-making process.

CHAPTER 9

The Land-Managed City

Up to now we have shown how man in his search for privacy uses the car to flee to sprawling suburbs, and in the process destroys the city and access to the integrated community. We have shown that man does not engage in these activities just because of a love affair with the automobile, the honest need for privacy or the burning desire to be the responsible owner of a mortgaged home, but at least as much because he is pushed by the unrelenting forces of the social and economic institutions, particularly in the United States, into these patterns of choice.

In this chapter we explore a city that has a very high rate of growth, extensive car ownership, a good public transit system, little if any decay in its core and no significant sprawl at its outskirts. The city that managed this feat is Edmonton, the capital of the Canadian Province of Alberta, in the great Western Plains near the foot of the Rocky Mountains. This metropolitan area of half a million souls is a new city which has quadrupled its population since the end of the Second World War under the influence of oil and gas discoveries and the increasing exploitation of Canadian resources in the Far North. Oil was discovered just south of the city in 1947 and Edmonton is the major gateway to the Alaskan Highway and Canada's Yukon and Northwest Territories.

Today, Edmontonians own a great number of passenger cars. Their ownership rate in 1970 was 364 cars per 1,000 population, just 16 per cent below the average U.S. rate. This is comparable to the state of Louisiana and greater than six other U.S. states. The Edmonton car-ownership rate is the same as for the Province of Alberta as a whole, it is greater than for eight of the ten Canadian provinces and greater than for Canada as a whole, or any other country save the United States. Before anyone assumes that Edmonton's severe winters make cars useful only in the summer, and public transit thus a necessity in the winter, let it be noted that the public transportation system in Edmonton has no greater seasonal variations in ridership than the Boston system.

When we began our analysis, we assumed that the severe Edmonton winters were an explanatory factor for Edmonton's patterns. However, our analysis persuaded us otherwise, even though we did the bulk of our field work during a week in February when the temperature never got as high as − 10°C. Twenty years ago and longer, Edmontonians used their cars only sparingly during the cold winter months, but now, with special heating devices for battery and engine block, as well as 'plug-ins' at every home and in most parking lots, cars start as easily in cold as in warm weather. Mr MacDonald, the head of the Edmonton Transit System, told us that in earlier days the seasonal variations in ridership were so great that the city garage scheduled major overhaul jobs on the transit equipment for the summer and on the public works equipment for the winter, but today the seasonal variations have disappeared sufficiently for this scheduling to be no longer possible.

Edmonton's topography is perfect for sprawl. Situated on the bluffs above the North Saskatchewan River, which bisects the city from the southwest to the northeast, the area is a high plateau with very little roll. To neither the north, the south, the east nor the west are there any natural barriers which prevent the city from sprawling. Still it has not happened. Edmonton's postwar residential subdivisions are more densely developed than those of other North American cities. There are hardly any vacant lots in the built-up areas. Finally, speculators do not hold wide vacant expanses between the more recent subdivisions for 'future developments'.

Statistically the uniqueness of Edmonton is apparent if one compares the city to Calgary, Alberta's other major city, or to United States cities of comparable size and growth. Edmonton has not only a significantly higher population density, but also a far greater availability and usage of transit (Table 3).

What made Edmonton such a unique city? As we noted, its rugged sub-arctic climate alone is not the answer. Its development can be traced to fortuitous historical 'accidents' or 'coincidents' where every dark cloud had its silver lining, and to the willingness to engage in rigorous land management. At least for the last generation, the Province of Alberta and Edmonton have enjoyed honest government, which has

Table 3: *Availability and usage of transit during 1969 in the medium-sized cities of Canada and the United States which had the largest growth rates between 1940 and 1970*

City	1970 Population (in 1000s)	Average annual growth rate (1940–70)	1970 Population density per square mile	1969 Transit availability index[a]	1969 Transit usage index[b]
Edmonton, Alberta	416	5.1%[c]	4,500	94	87
Calgary, Alberta	375[d]	5.1%	2,500[d]	46	77
Phoenix, Arizona	581	7.6%	2,300	g	g
Tucson, Arizona	263[f]	6.9%	3,300[f]	g	g
San Jose, California	440[f]	6.4%	3,800[f]	g	g
El Paso, Texas	322	4.8%	2,700	h	62[h]
San Diego, California	693[f]	4.2%	3,300[f]	40	26
Houston, Texas	1,231[f]	4.0%	3,100[f]	g	g
Jacksonville, Florida	518[f]	3.7%	1,500[f]	16	26
Dallas, Texas	844	3.6%	3,200	51	38
San Antonio, Texas	654	3.2%	3,600	44	34

a. Transit availability index = annual transit vehicle revenue mileage/(1000) (city area in square miles).

b. Transit usage index = annual revenue passengers/city population.

c. 1941–70. d. 1969. e. 1941–69.

f. Urban part of the incorporated area only, as defined by the U.S. Census.

g. We were unable to obtain the required transit data to calculate the transit availability and usage indexes; however, none of these cities have transit systems which either in availability or usage are comparable to Edmonton's.

h. System operates only in part of El Paso. This part has 95,000 residents. No availability index could be calculated; usage index is based on a population of 95,000.

made public land management and planning effective tools of government. But this type of government has also implied a great deal of paternalism, a feature which many find oppressive.[1]

Edmonton as a permanent settlement had its beginnings in 1812, when, after a number of false starts, the Hudson's Bay Company established a post on the northern bank of the river. The post flourished, but hardly made Edmonton into a metropolis. By 1892, when Edmontonians incorporated as a town, its population was only 700. Still, these years left Edmonton with two incidents that would impact its future growth. Until 1870, the Hudson's Bay Company 'owned' vast territories of today's Canada. That year, in a 'deed of surrender', the Company signed over title to these lands to the newly formed Dominion. In return the Canadian government granted the Company, among other considerations, some 45,000 acres around its 120 posts. One of these grants was the 3,000-acre Hudson's Bay Reserve, an area of 2.5 by 1.5 miles just outside the then settled part of Edmonton and well within today's city limits.

The second impact on Edmonton's development was a rumor which turned out to be false. In 1881, the Canadian Pacific was building its mainline across Canada and through the Rocky Mountains. What was more natural than that they should follow the old fur-trader route through Edmonton and the gently sloping Yellowhead Pass? On this presumption, a land boom developed in Edmonton which quickly collapsed when the Canadian Pacific chose the steeper and more southerly route through Calgary and Kicking Horse Pass and doomed Edmonton's growth for the foreseeable future. Edmontonians were naturally disappointed, and if they cried 'politics', they were right. It was, however, not local politics that pitted the small western outpost at Edmonton against the equally small outpost at Calgary, but international politics. The Dominion government was worried about protecting the prairies' southern border from American exploitation and invasion! Still, the short boom brought sufficient settlers to the area to reinforce the need of Edmonton as a trading post.

The first railroad to reach the Edmonton area was a branch line of the Canadian Pacific, the Calgary Edmonton Railway. This road

1. Kenneth McNaiglet, *The History of Canada*, Praeger Publishers, New York, 1970, page 249.

was built in 1891. Since the line approached Edmonton from the south, it had to cross the steep bluffs of the North Saskatchewan River before it could enter the town. With this natural impediment, the railroad stopped its train just south of the river. This was sufficient incentive for a new community to arise, and Strathcona was born. Since Edmonton had fewer than 700 souls and it was eleven years until the river was bridged by a narrow-gauged railroad, fourteen years until a transcontinental railroad reached Edmonton directly from the East, and twenty-two years before the CPR crossed the river, it is not astonishing that a sizable new community arose south of the river. What is astonishing is Edmonton's survival north of the river; and not just survival, but survival as the primary nucleus of the area. Edmonton apparently survived this second blow because it had the Hudson's Bay Company. The Company was at once Edmonton's dominant merchant and land owner. Had the Company moved to the railhead, it might have lowered its shipping costs, but at the same time it would have reduced the value of its Edmonton land holdings to that of farmable land in the sticks. To preserve the value of these holdings, it was in the Company's interest to maintain the trading center north of the river. Naturally, this is conjecture, since we have no records of what went through the minds of the Company's officials when they found out that the CPR would stop south of the river. Still, there are some interesting facts. In 1892, one year after the CPR reached Strathcona, the Hudson's Bay Company built its new store at Jasper Avenue and 103rd Street in the heart of downtown Edmonton. To emphasize further Edmonton's desire to survive as a community, railhead or not, it was also in 1892 that the Board of Trade decided legally to incorporate Edmonton as a town. The new town contained a little over 2,000 acres and included the southern portion of the Hudson's Bay Reserve as well as land to the east of it.

With the railroad came growth. Settlers were streaming into the prairie section of the Northwest Territories, and Edmonton, surrounded by the richest farmland in Alberta, received its share of land-hungry farmers from the Eastern Provinces, the United States and Eastern Europe. Both the area and Edmonton prospered. In 1899, Strathcona incorporated. By 1901, Edmonton had a population of 2,600 and there were another 1,600 south of the river. In 1904, now a community of over 8,000 inhabitants, Edmonton incorporated as a city and doubled its land area. The city included now nearly the entire Reserve as well as land to the west and east of it.

By 1905, the prairies were populated enough to organize formally the Provinces of Saskatchewan and Alberta. For Edmonton's good fortune, this occurred just a few months after the publisher of the local paper had become the Dominion's Minister of the Interior. When it became time in Ottawa to designate a provisional capital as part of the federal act that created the Province, Edmonton won out over Calgary, even though the latter was larger and on the transcontinental railroad. The following year, the members of the provincial legislature, having been properly wined and dined by the residents of the provisional capital, made it the permanent one.

In November 1905, the Canadian Northern reached Edmonton by a direct route from Winnipeg and the east. Edmonton was now a railroad head and a provincial capital, and it boomed! In one short year between 1905 and 1906 alone, customs receipts as well as the volume of mail and express parcels increased by a full 80 per cent.

The 1906 Census gave Edmonton a population of over 11,000 up from 2,600 five years before. To this can be added nearly another 3,000 who resided in Strathcona. The area was booming and in dire need of utility services: water, sewage, electricity, telephone and transportation. But this was not the time for private firms to raise capital for municipal improvements. In 1904, the city had sold a franchise to a private street-railway promoter, but he lost his $10,000 of 'good faith' deposit when he did not build the promised line. Wall Street, and probably Toronto, had become weary of utilities, and especially transportation companies, that issued glowing prospectuses of 10 per cent and higher returns, when in fact all they could offer was watered stock. By 1905 and 1906, at least in the United States, the attitude became cautious, and by 1907, with the market crash and depression, there was just no private money for municipal improvements. Edmonton's boom had come a bit too late to make private companies eager to supply Alberta's capital with needed utility services. Still, Edmonton needed these services and what the private sector would not supply, the public sector did. Thus, today, Edmonton has not just municipal water and sewage service, but also municipal telephone, electric and transit service. Of the basic utilities, only gas is supplied by a private company. Since Edmonton built its

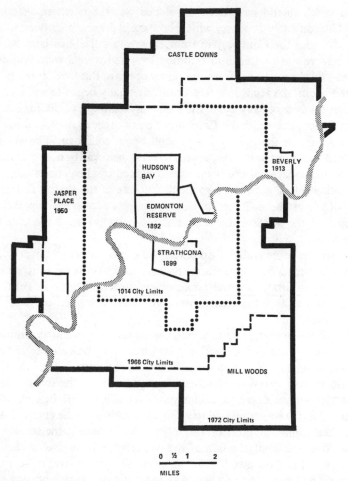

Map 8. *Edmonton's corporate boundaries (date after place name is year of incorporation)*

own utility services, it was in later years careful to prevent the city from growing to areas in which it would be too expensive to supply these services. But, in the early years, with the prevailing optimism, growth was hard to control. Land speculation was rampant. One big chunk of land which should have been developed was the northern section of the Hudson's Bay Reserve, which in 1904 had been incorporated into the city. But the Company did not choose to sell. Thus land beyond the reserve was plotted into building lots, and streets were laid out – at least on the map – far from the center of town. But then, at the height of the boom, the Hudson's Bay Company finally began to sell its land. In one sale, on 13 May 1912, the Company sold 1,543 building lots for over $4,300,000. From the Company's point of view, the sale came just in time, for in the next year the land boom collapsed. The era that opened the West was over, and the West was vastly over-expanded. While the collapse of the boom was triggered by the general economic conditions of the times and particularly those of the Prairie Provinces, the depth of the collapse in Edmonton was accelerated by the late release of the Reserve Land and the overextension of the city that preceded it.

When the boom ended, Edmonton had grown to a city of over 50,000 and had extended its boundaries to an area of over forty square miles. The town of Strathcona was amalgamated into Edmonton in 1912, and Edmonton as an integrated urban community extended to both sides of the river.

To tie the growing city together, the municipal government initiated transit operations in 1908 with six streetcars and twelve miles of track. In the beginning this service was limited to the north side of the river, but in 1910 service was expanded across the river to the south side. At first this service operated exclusively over a low-level bridge, which meant that the streetcars had to go down the bluffs to the river, cross it, and then climb the bluffs on the other side. Naturally, the service was slow. With the amalgamation of the two cities, a high-level bridge was constructed and open to service in 1913. The lower level of this two-level viaduct consisted of a roadway for vehicular traffic and two sidewalks for pedestrians, and the upper level of one track for the Canadian Pacific Railroad and two tracks for streetcars.

Edmonton's growth between the two world wars was slow but steady, and the population rose from 60,000 in 1916 to 92,000 by 1941. However, this growth came not in response to economic expansion, quite to the contrary. It came from natural increase and from the region's farmers who had homesteaded marginal land during the boom and were abandoning their inadequate holdings to find scarce employment in the city.

With the great optimism of the pre-First World War days and the limited growth between the wars, the transit route mileage that serviced the city in 1915 was still adequate in 1940. With one exception in these intervening years there was no expansion of the transit network, though some streetcar mileage was replaced with trolley buses and motor buses.

The streetcar tracks that were built prior to 1910 were laid out in populated areas and to serve a meat-packing plant. The lines built between 1910 and 1915, except for the high-level bridge route, were typical real-estate development lines, that is lines going through vacant lots in the hope of attracting home builders and buyers. Not surprisingly, route selection in Edmonton, as elsewhere, was to all appearances markedly assisted when by sheer coincidence council members had interests in specific properties along the line.[2]

Just as transit in the twenties and thirties was adequate, so was land. In fact, land within the forty-square-mile city was in strong oversupply. As one wit described it, the rectangular blocks of downtown Edmonton looked like a crossword puzzle half filled in. Meanwhile, the rest of the city was nearly empty prairie land, with a sprinkling of vegetable and dairy farms, shooting grounds, sloughs, skating ponds, thick brush, dumps and even an airport. With the city's slow growth much of the vacant land was considered worthless, and during the depression years of the 1930s reverted to the city through default of taxes.

In these years, city taxes and maybe the availability of the automobile caused some people to flee the city to an area known as Jasper Place. This community, just beyond Edmonton's inter-war city limits, had low taxes and few urban amenities. Its sole utility services consisted of electricity and unimproved streets. During the spring thaw and summer rains, a trip from Jasper Place to downtown Edmonton must have been quite a venture. The roads were impassable for cars, and until 1932 there was no transit. That year, the city, with its first motor-bus route, extended service to the city limits that abutted Jasper Place, but beyond that point one had to wade on foot through the mud of the unimproved streets.

2. J. G. MacGregor, *Edmonton – A History*, M. G. Hurtig Publishers, Edmonton, 1967, page 191.

In Edmonton, with its deep frost and long thaws, paved streets are a necessity for year-round vehicular service. It makes little difference if the vehicles are horse-drawn wagons or motor cars. Thus, Edmonton began to pave its streets early. By 1914, Edmonton, with about 400 miles of roadway, had forty-six miles of paved street, far more than other North American cities of equal size. But then further street paving was reduced to a crawl, and in the next twenty-five years only an additional sixteen miles of paved streets were added.

After thirty years of minimal growth, Edmonton at the end of the Second World War was ready to make up for lost time. Here was the pent-up demand of the lean depression years, as well as the ready cash from forced wartime savings to satisfy it. In Edmonton's case, the latter was particularly significant, for during the war years, and especially after the attack on Pearl Harbor, Edmonton had been buzzing. It was the gateway for the overland route to Alaska, which suddenly had become strategically important. Through Edmonton streamed the American and Canadian contractors that built the over 1,000-mile-long Alaskan Highway in the record time of nine months, followed later by the supplies that were being shipped to Alaska. In addition, Edmonton was a refueling stop for all air traffic that went to Alaska and from there to Russia. Through Edmonton moved every one of the 1,500 fighter planes the United States delivered to the Soviet Union under the lend-lease agreements.

While Edmonton's civilian economy expanded during the early post-war years, like that of every other unscathed city of the victorious allies, the expansion was really not a very convincing one, since there were no long-term prospects to support it. But in 1947, all this changed radically for the Province of Alberta and Edmonton.

That year oil was discovered in the Leduc oil fields south of Edmonton. The discovery was the result of many years of intensive exploration, and though the Leduc fields were important in themselves, they were only the forerunner of other oil and natural-gas fields to the south, north and northwest of Edmonton. These discoveries changed the economy of Alberta drastically. Up to that time Alberta had been a relatively poor debt-ridden province whose economy was based on wheat, a product that was not only subject to the vagaries of the weather, but also to the equally unpredictable prices of the world wheat market. Now Alberta could base its economy on oil and natural gas, whose production was not subject to the weather and for which the world has had so far an insatiable appetite. While in the 1920s Canada imported 95 per cent of her petroleum requirements, today Canada is not only self-sufficient but an exporter of oil and natural gas, with Alberta supplying two-thirds of Canada's petroleum production.

The poor Province of Alberta became one of Canada's richest, and today alone with the Provinces of Ontario and British Columbia receives no equalization payments from the federal treasury. The main revenue sources of Alberta's Provincial Government are the royalty payments of the oil and gas producers. In 1968 these amounted to 46 per cent of the Province's entire net general revenues. In the other provinces, this income source amounts to a bare 4 per cent of the net general revenues.[3]

After 1947, Alberta and Edmonton were booming again and really have not yet stopped. But these new economic expansions differed from the early one, not least with regard to the function of government. The intervening hard years had changed the public attitude towards its fellow men and government. Where once the public believed in the maxim 'every one for himself, and charitable dole for the truly "deserving poor"', now there existed a welfare-state attitude, where everyone is entitled by right to a minimum share of the economic pie. Under these changed circumstances, government planning and balancing for the common weal became not just accepted, but expected practice.

Edmonton, in these second years of expansion, needed careful public planning if it was not to scatter and sprawl to the four winds, like it had before, or like the booming cities south of the border. Since the discovery of oil barely twenty-five years ago, Edmonton has doubled its population and doubled it again, and today is still growing at better than 3 per cent per annum in spite of sharply dropping birth rates (Table 4).

Luckily for Edmonton, the city fathers not only recognized that they had to act in good times, when there are choices, with even more vigor than in hard times, but to their everlasting credit they also knew how to act.

3. *Canada Year Book 1970–71*, Dominion Bureau of Statistics, Ottawa, pages 1163–4.

As we have noted, the city contained plenty of vacant land, and through the tax foreclosures of the lean years the city owned much of it. There was so much vacant land in the city that the population grew to over 250,000, that is more than doubled, before the city annexed any

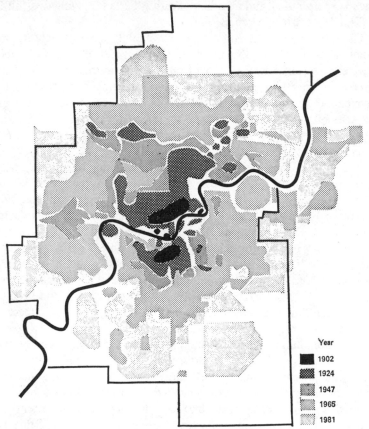

Year

■ 1902
▨ 1924
▨ 1947
▨ 1965
░ 1981

Map 9. *Edmonton's general plan for urban development 1902–81*

major new areas, even though two-thirds of all households were in single-family dwellings.

The city managed this growth without sprawling by a carefully conceived and executed land policy. First, all tax land that was sold by the city was sold subject to building commitments. This effectively dampened land speculation. Secondly, the city placed on sale first the vacant land nearest the center. The effect of this policy became quickly apparent on such desolate tracts as the Hudson's Bay Reserve land in the heart of the corporate city. In 1941, nearly thirty years after its public sale, not quite 4,000 persons lived there, by 1951 more than 10,000 called the area their home, and in 1956 it was nearly 15,000. Since then the number of residents has remained relatively stable.

Table 4: Population of Edmonton

	City	Metropolitan area
1941	93,924	98,770
1946	113,116	121,000
1951	159,631	176,000
1956	227,381	254,800
1961	281,027	337,568
1966	376,925	401,299
1970	429,376	457,566

Source: D. David O'Neil: *Metropolitan Edmonton Population: 1946–1970*, The City of Edmonton Planning Department Research Branch, May 1971, Table 22.

Finally, when the city opened up areas which consisted mainly of paper streets, the subdivisions were replotted from the regular rectangular grid to curves and crescents, deadend streets and service roads. This pattern discourages cars from straying off the straight-line arterial roads to find shortcuts through residential subdivisions. Thus Edmonton, earlier than most cities in North America, had residential street patterns that channeled the private automobile.

While Edmonton planned for the automobile, it never considered the private car the only means of urban transportation. Wherever an area was opened up for development, it was also furnished with transit service. This steady extension of service gave Edmonton by 1960 approximately four times the route mileage that had served the city between the two world wars (Table 5).

The system also converted from streetcars to trolley buses and motor buses. This conversion was completed by 1951, with the trolley buses operating on the so-called 'Central System' or the high passenger-density routes, and the motor buses serving the low-density routes of the 'Feeder System'. By 1960, the route net was sufficiently dense for 93 per cent of all Edmontonians to live within a quarter mile of a transit

Table 5: Edmonton transit mileage

Year	Round trip route mileage[1]
1920	56
1940	58
1950	109
1955	155
1960	214
1964	440
1971	449

1. The one-way or 'street' mileage is approximately half as much, but harder to estimate since most bus routes at the end of their runs in the outlying areas form one-way loops, along which they discharge out-bound passengers and pick up in-bound passengers.
Source: Edmonton Transit System.

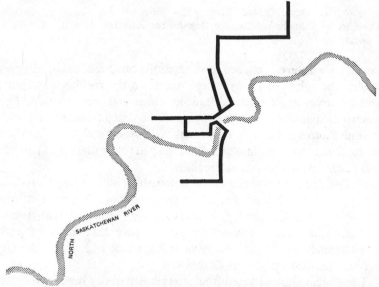

Map 10. *Edmonton's transit system. Daytime transit service, January 1910*

route, and 99 per cent within a third of a mile. The service was frequent. On every route there was a bus at least every thirty minutes, and during peak hours the frequency was as high as every three minutes along some of the central routes.

In 1960, if one looked backward through the past history of the system, the financial conditions looked good. The early transit system had been a steady loser of money, as the streetcars careened past the city's empty lots and wide open spaces. But the bulge in wartime ridership, together with wage freezes, had put the system finally on a sound

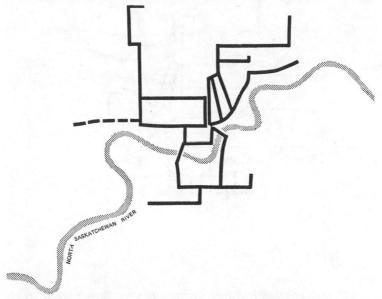

Map 11. *Edmonton's transit system. Daytime transit service, January 1938*

basis, though the fares were just 5 cents. During the fifties, with rising wages and other costs, the fares rose to 15 cents cash or eight tickets for $1. This was sufficient to turn the system's lifetime deficit balance with the City of Edmonton into a credit balance, even though ridership had declined steadily since the late forties.[4]

4. D. L. MacDonald, *Report of the Present Operations of the Edmonton Transit System with a View to Determining a Policy for the Future Operation of the System*, 24 August 1961, page 3.

One plus in the finances of the Edmonton Transit System (ETS) is the fact that it enjoys a monopoly position for supplying bus service within the city. ETS, then as well as now, is the only company that is permitted to charter buses or transport school children within the confines of the city. Such rather lucrative extra services often spell the difference between financial failure and success of transit companies. Especially in recent years ETS has been quite aggressive in maintaining

Map 12. *Edmonton's transit system. Daytime transit service, September 1951*

these services, and in 1971 nearly 12 per cent of its revenue came from these non-transit services. The importance of charter service, however, goes beyond the revenue they generate. They are also a marketing device. Frequently the first acquaintance a potential customer makes with the system is a chartered bus trip, particularly in a city like Edmonton, where new migrants and residents arrive daily from cities and towns with little or no transit service.

While in the early 1960s ETS's financial backward look was rosy, its future potential was not. Not only was ridership declining, but the routes centered on downtown, Jasper Avenue and the old Southside business district along Whyte Avenue, and provided only limited service to the rapidly growing outlying commercial and industrial centers. While transit handled 35 per cent of the work trips to and from the central area, it handled half this percentage, 17 per cent, of all other work trips.[5]

Map 13. *Edmonton's transit system. Daytime transit service, January 1966*

Of the non-work trips, transit handled 20 per cent, with no significant difference if the trips were to downtown or other parts of the metropolitan area. Also, to respond to the automobile, the city was planning a nearly 'classical' freeway system, consisting of an inner belt, radial spokes and a circumference highway. The inner belt would place a noose, $1\frac{1}{4}$ miles in diameter, around the downtown area.

5. *Metropolitan Area Transportation Study of 1961*, Vol. I, page 25.

The transit system responded to this challenge by revamping and sharply increasing the system's route structures. Instead of operating feeder buses in the outlying areas and requiring passengers to transfer to the main-route trolley-bus system to go downtown, the feeders became express buses to downtown after completing their feeder loop. This avoided transferring for passengers going downtown, certainly a welcome improvement particularly on sub-sub-zero days. In addition, 'ring' routes were introduced both on the north and south sides of the city to facilitate trip-making which was not downtown-oriented. None of these changes had any direct effect on the fares the passengers were charged, since Edmonton never used zone fare and has issued free transfers since 1909.

Still, rising costs and the doubling of route mileage, from 214 miles in 1960 to 449 miles in 1971, required a raising of the basic fares to 20 cents cash or seven rides for $1 in 1962, and to 25 cents cash or five rides for $1 in 1967. With the institution of these higher fares, ETS began issuing monthly transit passes for $10. These passes permit unlimited riding on the buses. Since the cost of the passes is equal to fifty transit tickets, a pass pays only if it is used for other trips besides the ride to and from work five days a week. As an aside, these passes reveal the imaginative and highly pragmatic attitude of the transit system. Since it is extremely costly, if not downright impossible, to control the use of passes, they are transferable, except that a rider must keep the pass in his possession throughout the trip. They cannot be bought from the bus drivers, but are sold at six locations and by mail. In 1971, ETS sold on the average 5,600 passes, or to approximately 2 per cent of the eligible population. The 'eligible' population excludes the children, who get rides for 15 cents, and the elderly, who can buy a lifetime pass for $5. With these measures, ridership and revenue have steadily increased since 1963 (Table 6), but the measures also increased the cost of transit operation, and the system is now operating at a net loss, which in 1970 amounted to $1.3 million. For every $1 of revenue, the system had expenditures, including interest and depreciation, of $1.17.

Part of the increased costs that were not offset by increased revenue arose because Edmonton was growing. During the early 1960s, the two abutting communities of Beverly and Jasper Place were incorporated into the city, and transit service was extended to the newly annexed areas. The residents of these communities could now ride the transit system from their homes to downtown for the same fare, which before required them to find additional transportation beyond the city limits.

Table 6: Edmonton transit system: Passengers, revenues and expenditures

	Passengers[1] (in millions)	Revenues ($000s)	Expenditures ($000s)	Surplus/loss ($000s)
1950	37.0	2,654	2,526	+128
1955	34.7	3,189	3,049	+140
1960	28.2	3,487	3,720	−233
1961	27.2	3,397	3,905	−508
1962	27.8	3,826	4,146	−321
1963	27.0	3,841	4,378	−536
1964	28.0	3,985	4,773	−789
1965	31.6	4,422	5,378	−956
1966	33.1	4,778	5,869	−1,091
1967	34.4	5,152	6,640	−1,486
1968	34.9	6,873	7,150	−824
1969	35.2	7,143	7,902	−1,128
1970	38.5	7,694	8,559	−1,328

Source: Annual Reports of the City of Edmonton.

1. Includes only transit passengers, does not include school bus or charter passengers. Revenues and expenditures are for total system operations.
Source: Annual Reports of the City of Edmonton.

Furthermore, though we have no hard data, we can assume that the people who had moved to Jasper Place and Beverly while working in the city were people who relied for their transportation needs primarily on their cars, thus were less prone to use transit than residents of neighborhoods that were developed as part of the city. Thus, these annexations required the transit system to extend its vehicle mileage quite out of proportion to the increase in ridership or revenues. But then it is the function of urban transportation to bind the city together, not to be a profit-making enterprise – and Edmonton apparently recognizes this.

Another reason for the growth of the Edmonton Transit System is the city's failure to build the proposed freeway net and particularly the inner belt. Canada, unlike the United States, has no special federal aid program for the construction of freeways. Lacking such a program, it is never cheaper for a municipality to build a freeway than a lesser road. Thus alternatives to freeways were carefully considered, particularly in Edmonton.

Due to Edmonton's postwar land policy and high growth rate, little urban decay developed in the downtown area. While the neighborhoods near downtown aged in Edmonton as elsewhere, the growing central business area supplied the capital to tear down decaying residential units and use the land for commercial buildings and apartment houses. Also, the city assesses land high enough and land improvements low enough to prevent effectively unimproved land from being held for speculation or used as parking lots for any lengthy period of time. All these pressures increased the value of downtown land and real estate, thus effectively increasing the cost of constructing freeways. Meanwhile, the detrimental impact of freeways on United States cities did not escape the Edmonton citizenry, and in 1971 the City Council instructed the Planning Department to do a study 'on the possible deleterious effects of freeways on adjoining residential lands and make recommendations to reduce such effects to a minimum'.[6]

Even with a good bus and trolley system, the downtown streets of Edmonton will in the long run be unable to carry the expected traffic of the growing city. To solve this problem, Edmonton is now planning a rapid transit system combined with limited freeway mileage. By aggressively annexing new land to the city and rigorously managing land use and development within the city, Edmonton, in cooperation with the regional and provincial planning authorities, has discouraged sprawl and leapfrogging. Even so, these policies have not been 100 per cent effective. There are still a few pockets of sprawl just beyond the city limits. More ominously, in the late sixties and early seventies, small communities twenty-five to sixty miles from Edmonton began to grow at an alarming rate. Here developers began to build housing for Edmonton workers because the city's Planning Department had become rough on poor-quality development and lot prices had climbed too high.

6. City Council resolution on 8 February 1971.

The long-term effects of these developments did not escape the Edmonton City Council and Planning Department, and their response showed again the city's need and willingness for land planning. Land speculation had to be stopped, and there was only one way in which it could be stopped. The city had to furnish private and commercial home builders with land at reasonable prices. By the 1960s, the tax land the city acquired during the great depression had all been developed.

To acquire new land and, so to speak, rebuild its land bank, the city, with the help of the Province, quietly acquired over a six weeks period in 1970 options to Mill Woods, a nine-square-mile area abutting the city to the southeast. The deal was managed so 'quietly' that, we are told, only six persons knew that the options were sought for the city's land bank. According to the city's Project Director, the area will be developed as nine distinct communities, with a 'high degree of integration of local facilities, emphasizing pedestrian movement and environmental factors'.[7] The first lots were put up for sale in 1971 and the city expects it will be well into the 1980s before all of Mill Woods is developed.

One effect of this land-bank scheme was the decision by the largest private real-estate developer, BACM Industries, to begin immediately with the systematic development of their nine and a half square mile area, Castle Downs, on the city's north side. Further delays cannot raise the value of this land as long as the city has land to offer at Mill Woods and can thus effectively determine the value of building lots in Edmonton. Not surprisingly, after the city offered the first lots at Mill Woods for about $5,200. BACM set the offering price of its first 500 serviced lots between $5,000 and $6,000.

Obviously, the optioning of vacant land for a land bank must be done very quietly or the value of the land jumps immediately. Also, the location is determined by what is available rather than by what fits best into a master plan. From the amalgamation of Edmonton and Strathcona in 1912 until 1972, the city developed more or less along a south-west to northeast axis, and all master planning for the next twenty-five years had assumed that this general trend would continue. But with the decision to develop Mill Woods to a population of 120,000 and Castle Downs to a population of 100,000, the next two decades will see the expansion of the city on a north-by-west to south-by-east axis. This

7. *Edmonton Journal*, 29 January 1972, page 67.

shift in expected growth will require a major rethinking of the city's general plan for transportation and other utility facilities.

This rethinking is particularly critical for the Mill Woods area, which is separated from the city's other general urban areas by an industrial belt one to two miles wide. To give the area land-bank leverage, the lots must not just be inexpensive but also well serviced with all utilities, including transportation. We surmise that the quiet assembling of the Mill Woods options went as smoothly as it did because no one thought the city would try to assemble a land bank in *that* direction.

The distance from Mill Woods to downtown is eight to twelve miles, thus bus service will be slow and expensive. Should the city decide to charge extra for these very long rides, then the Mill Woods area will become even more isolated from the rest of Edmonton than it already is. On the other hand, the area is easily serviced by rapid transit. There is a railroad right-of-way that runs from downtown to within less than a mile of Mill Woods, and the area between the right-of-way and Mill Woods is not built up. The only drawback to the scheme is that for the time being there will be little traffic in and out of Mill Woods, and all past traffic studies indicate that the 'proper' location for rapid transit on the south side is about four miles to the west of Mill Woods.

In light of these changes, Edmonton is just now, in 1972, reworking its long-range transportation plan. We shall watch with interest how Edmontonians will employ their transportation resources to meet their land-development objectives.

It is our hypothesis that sprawl and auto dependency generates alienation. Thus the question arises, has Edmonton with its land-use and transportation policies achieved a socially more integrated community with less alienation? We do not know the answer to this question. A comparative analysis would have carried us well beyond the scope of this book. As we mentioned, some find the paternalism of Alberta and Edmonton oppressive, and books like the *Harvard Student Guide to Travel in North America* are anything but enthusiastic about the city. They consider it straight and dull. Like every city, Edmonton has its local boosters, but there are others who claim that over-all Calgarians are even more enthusiastic about their city. Still, these are just surface reactions and pretty meaningless. An in-depth study does not exist and in its absence we must pass the question.

CHAPTER 10

A Look Ahead

In this century of phenomenal new technologies, it is natural to look to engineers and scientists in the hope that on their drawing boards and in their laboratories there might be the magic black box that can solve the urban access problem.

The drawing boards and laboratories are by no means empty, and the next few decades will see the introduction of many new techniques into urban transportation systems. Without any serious reservation we can predict that the cars of the 1990s will be considerably less polluting than those of today. Their engines will be more fuel-efficient and there may be even electric-powered cars that are more than toys. The cars of tomorrow will be quieter and hopefully safer; they may even be easier to maintain. But such technological improvements will not ease the access problem. With one possible exception, there is nothing in the wind that will make driving a car easier or that will change significantly the proportion of drivers to non-drivers. There are no black boxes like the electric starters or the automatic transmissions which can convince large segments of the population that they too can master the art of driving.

Dual-mode systems are the one possible exception that might make driving easier. 'Dual mode' refers to a whole host of concepts which all have one characteristic in common. The vehicle can be driven on any street or highway like an ordinary car, bus or truck, but in addition it can be automatically controlled along a guideway. The advantage of a dual-mode car over a conventional one is its ability to travel at higher than freeway speeds along the guideways. The vehicles can also follow each other safely at closer distances than driver-controlled cars. This increases the number of vehicles that can use a single traffic lane.

If dual-mode systems are ever built – their economy is somewhat doubtful – they may have considerable effect on urban access. It is possible that many people who today are afraid to drive on the freeways would be willing to drive their cars onto a dual-mode guideway. This willingness will be mainly a function of the driving skills needed to enter and leave the guideways. Since the systems are still very much in the study, rather than building, stages, it is not known if entering and leaving the guideways will require greater or lesser driving skills than coping with freeway traffic. Certainly, once on the guideway travel will be faster and less tiring than on freeways. As long as the car is on the guideway, the 'driver' has nothing to do. Thus commuters who travel by 'dual mode' may be more willing to commute over longer distances than the auto drivers on the freeways. If this should happen, dual-mode systems would cause increased sprawl and a further dispersion of activities. While dual mode may give some drivers greater access, the increased sprawl represents a further loss in access for the rest of the population.

One class of new systems that tries to attack the access problem directly is the Personal Rapid Transit (PRT) systems. These systems consist of small driverless vehicles operating on a network of exclusive guideways which take passengers non-stop between stations. The passenger enters these vehicles at a station and, by pressing a button on a panel, informs the system of the station he desires to go to. The vehicle then threads through the guideways to the desired station. In some versions, the vehicles are suspended from overhead monorails, in others they ride on conventional rails or similar guideways that support the vehicle from underneath.

The PRT systems are certainly appealing. Anyone who is physically able to ride a bus, streetcar or subway could ride a PRT. If the stations have elevators, even a person unable to mount the steps to a bus could use a PRT, since all the proposed designs use 'high' platforms, like the subways. Even though the PRTs are very appealing as a concept, we doubt they will ever become important elements of the urban transportation picture. Their drawbacks are economic. PRT systems either have very low capacity, or require a lot of space, the city's most precious resource. If there are too many cars on the network, queues quickly begin to form. Although the passenger would not get caught in an automobile jam, he could be caught in a mammoth traffic jam of PRT vehicles. Computer simulations have shown that, even on very simple networks with relatively few cars, jams can occur in rather rapid order. To avoid these jams, vehicles must be scheduled. This means the passenger no longer could step into the vehicle and press a button for his destination, but would have to press a button on the station platform and wait until a vehicle came along that was willing to take him to his destination. Under this scheme, waiting passengers at a station would not be served in the order they pressed the buttons, but in the order which is most efficient for the system to serve them. If passengers have to wait anyway, they might as well travel together, and soon it becomes apparent that the system could carry even more passengers if each car were not dispatched separately but if cars were coupled into trains. The system could be even more efficient and serve more people at lower costs if the trains of some passengers stopped en route, and finally, if some of the passengers changed trains in the course of their journey. After the designers, builders, planners and buyers of PRT systems consider all these factors, a practical system looks in the end remarkably like a modern subway system with centrally controlled dispatching and automatic controls.

In the United States, the federal government is building a prototype PRT system in Morgantown, West Virginia, to try out the concept in actual passenger service. At this writing the system is not yet operational, but is already 200 per cent over the original cost estimates. The system also has only three stations, which makes us wonder what this prototype will prove.

Many transportation planners have considered PRTs as the ideal solution for transporting passengers around the major airports, where the distances are too great for walking. But even in this rather restricted environment, pure PRT systems have not been able to meet the capacity requirements. The most extensive studies of PRT systems for this use were made in connection with the planning and building of the new Dallas/Fort Worth Airport that opened in 1973. This airport, in the wide open spaces of Texas, is by far the largest commercial airfield and terminal complex anywhere. Originally, the designers had planned to move all connecting passengers from their arrival to their departure gates with a PRT system. This plan was abandoned when no PRT design could guarantee to handle all these passengers within twenty minutes during peak hours. The system that was finally built consists of small automatic trains and requires some airline passengers to transfer in their journey from one airline gate to another.

PRT systems will probably remain the dream of designers and an amusement-park curiosity rather than become urban transit systems. Still, the general principles they embody – the automatic vehicle controls, switching on demand and optimizing traffic flow – are some of the new control technologies which will be incorporated in the more standard transportation systems, such as subways, buses and traffic signals.

With these control devices we can expect much less fanciful but more effective traffic improvements: special lanes for buses, priority entering of freeways by buses, traffic lights that turn green when a bus is approaching and automatically controlled subway trains. This general technology can also be used to improve the dispatching of radio-controlled taxicabs and possibly the routing of minibuses according to demand, the so-called dial-a-ride or dial-a-bus systems.

Most of these new devices are sold to the public as cost savers or as solutions to the congestion problem. Cost savers they may be, but solutions to the congestion or access problem they are not. If land use and general travel demand is not controlled, traffic will always pile up until there is a congestion problem. The streetcar, the subway, the auto and the truck were all billed as solutions to the congestion problem. But experience has shown just how successful these 'solutions' were.

It is really not astonishing that new technology has no effective answer to the urban transportation problem, for the old technology did not create it. Boston and Edmonton use identical technology. Both cities have cars, trolley buses and motor buses of identical or nearly identical make. Boston, in addition, has streetcars and subways. This is not the difference between the two cities. Boston and Edmonton differ in the organization of transportation and the control of land use. It is through these means that the urban transportation problem will be solved or at least alleviated. But first there must be agreement on the problem that should be solved.

Most transportation proposals consider congestion and the speed of travel the two primary problems. Nearly every transportation invention has been hailed as the panacea for these problems. Only those as benign as the Prussian King have dared to question these maxims. Traffic congestion basically is full utilization of the transport facilities, and thus is not necessarily a problem. If transport facilities are never congested, they are always underutilized. Congestion becomes a social and economic problem only when it delays travel so that a substantial number of trips are not made or are diverted to other localities. Likewise, if the speed of travel is enhanced, people just travel further to absorb the time that is available to them for travel, or use travel time to lower the ground rents for housing and plant facilities. Thus, as long as the benefits of highway and transit proposals are measured by the decrease in travel time they furnish, the present pattern of urban sprawl and segregation will be reinforced.

The problem of modern urban transportation is not congestion or speed, but access. Equal access to all, or nearly all, can be an urban reality if transportation and land-use projects are evaluated and ranked by the access they offer. In practical terms this implies that public transit would be given priority over private transportation, and that land-use patterns would be arranged to minimize travel distances.

Priority of public transportation over private transportation appears to be justified because a city too large for walking is, without public transit, divided into those with and those without access. It makes no difference if private transportation is by car, motorcycle, motor scooter, bicycle or horse-drawn surrey. All these systems offer good-to-excellent access to their owner-drivers, but they offer little or no access to the rest of the population, and this rest, even in the United States, is a majority. Private transportation, by whatever means, is thus a luxury supplement to public transportation, and public planning and financing should reflect this.

To reorient metropolitan areas from increased reliance on private transportation to increased reliance on public transportation, it is first necessary to furnish the metropolitan area with public transportation. Transit should be available within walking distance anywhere within the metropolitan area. Where transit exists now it should be maintained, where it is lacking transit routes should be established. But transit does not really exist if there is a bus once an hour and no one knows how far behind or ahead of schedule. Transit needs to be frequent, at least every 30 minutes during the day and evening, and maybe even every 15 minutes. More than one study has shown that with headways larger than 15 minutes there is a marked drop in ridership. The less frequent the service, the more important that it is punctual and comfortable. If there is a bus or train every 2 or 3 minutes, people seem to mind far less if they must stand, or if the vehicle is not quite on schedule, than if the bus or train comes only every 15, 20 or 30 minutes. If riders must plan their day around infrequent transport schedules, they feel that at a minimum the service should operate when it is scheduled to operate.

Dense, frequent networks are not sufficient to make transit the primary urban transportation mode. Transit must also be inexpensive. Travel by transit ought to be cheaper than travel by car. The marginal price of a transit trip ought to be less than the marginal price of a car trip. People will always desire to own cars for recreational travel, to go to the mountains, to the seashore, for family outings, for hauling of parcels and packages, and as mobile 'private bedrooms'. Thus for travel by transit to be less expensive than travel by car, the out-of-pocket costs of taking transit must be less than driving a car a few miles in the urban area. Free transit, which is now being advocated by many, meets this criterion. But in many respects only barely. Auto drivers perceive their out-of-pocket costs to be limited to the gasoline they use, and often this expense is forgotten. People pay for gas only when they finally drive up to a gas station after many short trips, and those with charge cards pay even less frequently.

Free transit by itself has also other drawbacks. Someone must pay for the cost of transit. While, as we have seen, most of the benefits of urban travel accrue to others than the traveler, some of the benefits do accrue to the travelers, and to this extent they might just as well pay for them. However, to make the traveler pay for each trip separately, and maybe even for the 'privilege' of transferring, is ridiculous. It seems to us that the best way of charging the transit traveler is by the time he desires to have the system available to him. Thus he should be able to buy passes by the hour, day, week, month or even year, and these passes should entitle him during this period to an unlimited number of rides. The passes should be good system-wide so that no one area of the community is economically less accessible, except in time, than any other area.

If it costs money to ride transit, then those who choose to use private transportation, be it a car, a motorcycle and maybe even a bicycle, should pay more than the transit rider. Thus persons who wish to enter the metropolitan area with these vehicles, or store and drive them in the area, should also have to buy time-limited passes. The charge for these passes should be equal to one transit pass for each seat in the vehicle, plus a surcharge. This way it would never be cheaper to travel by private transportation than transit.

A serious commitment to give transit priority over private transportation requires that travel by transit be generally as fast as travel by private transportation. Where road traffic is uncongested, transit can use the same road network as all other road traffic. In these areas, the bus provides the most economical and still adequate form of public transportation. Where the road network is crowded with trucks and private cars, transit needs its own right-of-way. If the needs are over an extended area, a tracked train system like a subway is often the best solution. If the high-congestion area is relatively small, or if the congestion points are widely distributed, a special bus road may be the answer. These are roads which are limited to buses and they can be either below ground, at street level or elevated. The advantage of this scheme is the ability of the vehicles, the buses, to travel both on the special bus roads and the common road network. The disadvantage compared to subways is the lower capacity of the system. A single bus lane cannot handle as much passenger traffic as a single subway track and also requires more space.

If the urban street and arterial network is unable to accommodate the road traffic, even with the transit improvements, then the metropolitan area requires more highways, that is, greater road capacity. In many cases, limited access roads such as parkways and expressways are the most efficient solution to this problem, and highly preferable to extensive street widening and the destruction of the tree-lined medians along the city boulevards. But if these highways are built, they should not be turned over to the private automobile traffic, or worse yet to the exclusive use of the private car; rather they should provide speedy travel to those vehicles which are most essential to the health of the urban area, the bus and the truck. We advocate these transportation improvements, because they increase access, but the political and economic impetus for such improvements may well be generated by the desire to conserve fuel.

Many city and transportation planners, as well as other futurists, have long recognized that one solution to urban traffic is not to travel. Thus these people have spoken hopefully of the new communication devices as relievers of traffic. The telephone may have contributed to the lessening of traffic, and the radio, television and dataphone all in their time have been so hailed. Even if all these devices are in some respect relievers of traffic, on the whole they generate more traffic than they avoid. There is little doubt that the future will see further communication improvements and extensions such as videophones, closed-circuit and cable television, two- and three-dimensional remote computer displays, and maybe even 'tele-odors'. Still, none of these devices will in the long run reduce the need for travel. Under no reasonable scenario for the future, unless there is a recombining of the residential/production unit, can we imagine that the people of tomorrow will make fewer trips than those of today. All that can reasonably be planned for is more, not less, trip-making. Thus whatever is done, no reduction in extrinsic or intrinsic trip-making should be expected. Still this does not mean that urban travel must necessarily increase. While people in the future will make more trips than today, particularly if public transit becomes readily available, their travel measured in distance need not increase, but can efficiently and effectively be decreased through more rational land use.

To minimize travel mileage, large tracts of land should not be reserved for any single type of activity. Large industrial parks, central business districts, regional shopping centers, office complexes and large areas devoted to residential use, worse yet, large areas devoted to a single type of residential use, are all enormous generators of travel mileage and with it air pollution. A quiet residential metropolitan suburb where all houses are on two-, three- and four-acre lots generates an enormous amount of travel mileage and travel-connected pollution for the activities it contains, even if there are hardly any cars on its quiet neighborhood streets. Because of their dispersal, the services these homes require must be trucked over greater distances, and the residents must travel greater distances to satisfy their work, shopping, cultural and recreational requirements than if the homes were interspersed with homes on smaller lots, offices, plants, cultural and shopping facilities. In addition, the absorption of concentrated space for one particular activity requires uncounted other residents and businesses of the metropolitan area to travel further to bypass this enclave in the pursuit of their interests.

Land-use controls can be methods for locating residential, industrial, commercial, institutional and recreational properties in the spatial relations to one another which minimize travel distances. To be effective these controls need to be exercised not only within the metropolitan area but well beyond it to cover the entire region and perhaps the nation. The difficulties Edmonton has in controlling sprawl at the fringes are largely because their physical land-use controls do not extend over a wide enough area. If private auto traffic inside an urban area is discouraged through special charges, or in any other way, it is necessary to control the land use well beyond the restricted area to prevent sprawl at the fringes.

But land-use controls alone will not achieve these objectives; fiscal policies are also needed. Here a carrot and stick tax policy can help. People who move closer to their place of work should get a tax break. In 1964, the United States made moving expenses tax deductible if they were associated with a change of employment as long as the new place of work was at least thirty miles further from the old residence than the previous place of work. Because of the thirty-mile clause, the rule did not really apply to those who changed jobs within a metropolitan area. To make quite sure that it would not affect adversely even longer local commuter trips, the minimum distance was increased to fifty miles in 1969. It would be far better for the relief of urban transportation and congestion, a frequently stated objective of the U.S. government, if *all* moves that reduce the commute distance were tax deductible. Tax-deductible moves should be the carrot and a special tax for excessive commuting the stick. Thus anyone who commutes over a minimum distance of ten or fifteen miles should pay a commute tax which increases exponentially as the distance of the commute increases.

In accordance with our hypothesis, urban transportation systems with sufficient mobility for the functioning of the urban economy cannot rely solely on user charges. Thus also the urban transportation which we propose. Even with the special charges for private transportation and excessive commuting it will not be self-supporting, but needs additional support from tax revenues. Since it is the requirement of the national economy that generates cities and the basic need for daily travel, the tax revenues to support urban transportation should come from a general tax on national economic activities.

Finally, if all the policies which we have outlined were instituted, a general reshaping of the metropolitan area would take place. The market forces, which in the rubber city lead to dispersion and segregation, would in the context of these policies become instruments of reconcentration and integration. Thus these forces might re-create the urban balance which existed for a fleeting moment early in the century; but hopefully now on a more stable and lasting basis.

Still, as the Edmonton example illustrates, urban transportation costs increase faster than the growth of the metropolitan area. The total bill for urban transportation is considerably more than twice as high for a metropolitan area of one million as for one of half a million. The excessively large metropolitan areas of New York, London, Paris, Tokyo, Chicago and Los Angeles have long ago passed the economies of large scale. This may even be true for metropolitan areas of as few as one or two million. Because of their sheer size, these areas can never expect to provide efficient access for all. The ultimate solution to the transportation problem in these areas cannot come from better transit and better land use alone. The size and the growth of the major metropolitan areas must be limited if one day they are not to drown in their traffic.

We have not discussed why cities grow, only how transportation shapes the growth of urban areas. Since we have not discussed the economic forces that generate urban growth, it is beyond the scope of this last chapter to discuss means to control and limit these economic forces – except for one note. As long as transportation was a scarce commodity, transportation furnished a limit to metropolitan growth. Today, transportation is no longer a scarce commodity. Though rising fuel costs may make transportation a less abundant commodity, it cannot be expected to become so scarce that it will represent again a natural governor on metropolitan growth and sprawl. Neither do such natural limits seem to arise from water and food supply, sewage, garbage and trash disposal. In the absence of these natural governors, national and possibly international social and economic policies must be devised as curbs to the unlimited expansion of metropolitan areas.

INDEX

About the Authors

Elliott Sclar is an economist who specializes in urban
development. He has worked extensively with community
groups and agencies in attempts to improve urban
transport. He is presently the chairman of the
Division of Urban Planning at Columbia University.
Elliott Sclar received his Ph.D. from Tufts University.

K. H. Schaeffer has been a Lutheran minister, a professor
of philosophy, a sampling statistician and, since 1952,
an operations analyst. He is a member of the Operations
Research Society, the Transportation Research Board, the
Philosophy of Science Association, and a past member of
the American Philosophical Association. K. H. Schaeffer
is currently on the staff of the U.S. Transportation
Systems Center in Cambridge, Massachusetts.